PLATES.

ILLUSTRATIONS IN TEXT.

(xiii)

The Schwenkfelders

in Pennsylvania

AMS PRESS
NEW YORK

The Schwenkfelders

in Pennsylvania,

A HISTORICAL SKETCH.

PART XII. OF A NARRATIVE AND CRITICAL HISTORY

PREPARED AT THE REQUEST OF

THE PENNSYLVANIA–GERMAN SOCIETY

BY

HOWARD WIEGNER KRIEBEL.

ILLUSTRATED BY JULIUS F. SACHSE, LITT.D.

LANCASTER, PA.
1904

Reprinted from the edition of Lancaster, 1904
First AMS EDITION published 1971
Manufactured in the United States of America

International Standard Book Number: 0-404-07219-4

Library of Congress Number 73-134413

AMS PRESS INC.
NEW YORK, N. Y. 10003

AN OFFERING OF THANKS TO GOD

FOR HIS UNSPEAKABLE GIFTS,

A TRIBUTE OF RESPECT

FOR THE EXAMPLE OF A PIOUS ANCESTRY,

A SLIGHT CONTRIBUTION OF MATERIAL FOR A

HISTORY OF GOD'S KINGDOM ON EARTH.

PREFACE.

THE following letter is offered by the author as a reason and apology for allowing his name to appear in the list of historians who have so well been telling the story of the Pennsylvania-Germans in the annals of the Pennsylvania-German Society.

" LEBANON, PA., NOV. 12, 1900.

PROF. H. W. KRIEBEL,
Pennsburg, Pa.,

My Dear Sir:

I am pleased to inform you that our Executive Committee at its recent meeting in Easton selected you to write a paper on the " Schwenkfelders " especially with regard to their history in this Commonwealth. * * * A declination under these circumstances would be a serious matter to us.

Sincerely yours,
H. M. M. RICHARDS, *Secretary*.

Thanks are hereby offered to the Society for esteeming the story of the Schwenkfelders worthy of a place in the critical History of Pennsylvania now being published by the Society, for the honor conferred in entrusting to the writer the preparation of such account, for the kindness and consideration uniformly shown him in his labors. A general acknowledgment of indebtedness is also due and hereby cheerfully made to the various institutions and individuals who have aided the writer in the prosecution of his study and research.

This sketch is in some measure at least a pioneer work and thus has not had the benefit of previous publications refined in the critic's crucible. Its shortcomings are painfully evident to the author but he hopes that they may not discredit the more fortunate features nor the subject itself. No claim is laid to originality. As a matter of fact almost every sentence may be traced to some original authority, almost exclusively German. An honest effort has been made by the writer to give facts faithfully as found, to avoid drawing inferences or flattering fancies of the imagination. Should some kind reader feel that undue prominence has been given in the sketch to the religious and doctrinal phase of life, it is hoped that a careful perusal of the whole will satisfy him that to eliminate this feature would be equal to taking the Prince of Denmark out of " Hamlet," Christian out of Bunyan's " Pilgrim's Progress " or Washington out of the " History of the American Revolution." Footnotes respecting translations or sources of information have been omitted because in most cases the material would be inaccessible to the general reader. Neither did it seem desirable to note the misstatements and misrepresentations made by various writers.

The initial letters at the beginning of each chapter are fac-simile reproductions from the manucript hymn-book written by Christopher Kriebel, 1765.

It is sincerely hoped that the present effort may induce a more thorough study of Schwenkfelder history and the publication of monographs on special phases of the subject. The reader will not forget that he is viewing the life of a simple country folk and that the thought so beautifully set forth in Gray's Elegy is still worthy of consideration.

> " Let not ambition mock their useful toil,
> Their homely joys and destiny obscure,
> Nor grandeur hear with a disdainful smile
> The short and simple annals of the poor."

EAST GREENVILLE, PA.,
January 19, 1904.

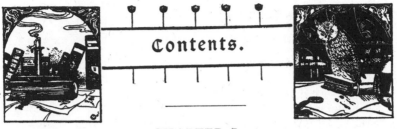

Contents.

(xi)

xii Contents.

SCHWENKFELDER HISTORIANS.

OSWALD KADELBACH.   CHESTER DAVID HARTRANFT.
1820-1882.   FRIEDRICH SCHNEIDER.
1806-1882.

CHAPTER I.

CASPER SCHWENKFELD.[1]

Wappen von Liegnitz.

CASPER SCHWENKFELD, the oldest child in a family of four, was born of Catholic parents at Ossig near Liegnitz in Silesia, Germany, 1490 (1489?), and died at Ulm, December 10, 1562. The family, which was of the nobility and could trace the story of its ancestry several hundred years, ended about two hundred years after his birth.

Taught by priests who bribed him with sugared cakes, he, as a Catholic, early learned to repeat his lessons of Romish praise and prayer; he later studied in Liegnitz and at Frankfurt, Cologne and other universities.

Having prepared himself for his station, though his general culture may perhaps have been somewhat limited, he, while yet a young man, entered upon the life of a courtier and as such served at several courts; first, at the

---

[1] Variations in the spelling of Schwenkfeld's name: Gaspar, Caspar, Casper, Chaspar, Gasper, Kaspar; Schwenckueld, Schwenckfeld, Schwenckfeldt, Schwenkfelt, Schwenckhfeldt, Schewenkfeldt, Schwenkfeld.

court of Duke Carl of Münsterberg, a grandson of King
Podiebrad of Bohemia, where the views of Huss were
upheld and probably impressed on his receptive heart;

TITLE PAGE OF ONE OF SCHWENKFELD'S EARLY LETTERS ADDRESSED
TO BISHOP OF BRESLAU JACOB V. SALZA.

later, at the court of Duke Friedrich II. of Liegnitz, as
Hofrat or aulic councilor.

During his courtier life, which lasted quite a number of
years, Schwenkfeld probably did not take a deep interest
in the Bible, but, God having touched his heart, he with-
drew from court life to Liegnitz where he preached and
taught. Here he became an intense student of the Bible,
theology, the Church Fathers and the Greek language.
When the advance waves of the Lutheran upheaval struck
Silesia, Schwenkfeld rejoiced; when Friedrich II. embraced the Reformation, Schwenkfeld heartily encouraged
him and threw his own whole life into the movement, thus
greatly aiding in the spread of the new light in Silesia,
for which he received the good wishes of Luther.

The want of harmony between the theories of Luther
and Schwenkfeld, recognizable in the two letters written
by the latter in 1524, became an open and endless discord
between the parties themselves a year later. Schwenkfeld
saw that he could not agree with Luther in reference to the
nature of Christ's presence in the Lord's Supper. Having
talked and prayed over the matter with his friends he,
after further earnest study and prayer, went with letters of
introduction to Bugenhagen and Justus Jonas at Witten-
berg for the purpose of laying his views before Luther
both orally and by books and manuscripts. A talk lasting
several days followed, after which Schwenkfeld went
home in good spirits, to receive later a fiery letter from
Luther in which, among other things, the charge is made
that either the writer, Luther, or Schwenkfeld must be the
bond-servant of the devil. The storm of persecution which
thus began to show itself was destined, under God's Providence, to blow about the heads of Schwenkfeld and his
followers for more than 200 years, and though on Penn's
soil a refuge was found in 1734, its after effects may be
seen and felt to this day. The system of doctrine which

Schwenkfeld had formulated at this time and which proved beyond doubt that he was a fearless, conscientious and profound thinker even then, was developed unaltered with the passing years and maintained unflinchingly in minutest detail to the hour of death.

Silesia at this time was budding into new life and a rich soil into which the seeds of the Reformation might drop lay ready. Schwenkfeld, although he had been repulsed by Luther, maintained his position by speech and pen both in public and private with the aid of his bosom friend, Crautwald. He thus won many adherents to his views and there was a promising prospect that Silesia, beginning at Liegnitz, would embrace the "Reformation by the Middle Way" as the movement under Schwenkfeld was called. Friedrich II. and nearly all the ministers of Liegnitz having embraced the doctrine, the University of Liegnitz was projected, partly organized and put into operation, soon to be smothered by adverse influences beyond the control of its friends. Opposing forces were at work at the same time, however. The publication of one of Schwenkfeld's tracts by Oecolampadius helped to increase the wrath and zeal of Luther and the Lutheran ministers against Schwenkfeld. The issue of Schwenkfeld's defense of his own views about the Lord's Supper without his consent or knowledge by Zwingli in Zurich in 1528 led the Bishop of Vienna to oppose Schwenkfeld in writing which in turn led King Ferdinand to serve notice on Friedrich of Liegnitz that he should punish the new teacher. To save his friends, Schwenkfeld upon this left home, voluntarily and not as an exile by the will of the duke, to live away from home and its comforts, from friends and kindred all the remaining days of his life. The letter of pardon which brought with it a chance to return to his home which was offered by the king, was not accepted since it would have implied that he should reconcile himself to the Church, its offices, regulations and sacraments, to teach only what the Church taught and to publish nothing without the knowledge and acceptance of the king.

Schwenkfeld lived thereafter in Strasburg, Nuremberg, Augsburg, Ulm and other important centers, besides visiting friends and staying temporarily in many of the free imperial cities of South Germany, persecution following him wherever he went. From Strasburg he was exiled in 1533; from Augsburg, compelled to withdraw in 1535; at Tübingen after a colloquy, peace and cessation from persecution were promised though not publicly proclaimed, 1535; at Ulm inquisition machinery was set in motion against him, happily set at rest, however, by the War of Smalcald. In 1558 he wrote that he was nowhere secure and that he could not move about without being in considerable danger. Decrees were issued against him, his books were confiscated and burned, his printers were forbidden to print, his booksellers, to sell his books. He was denounced in pulpit by priest and pastor, in church conference by almost every important gathering. Those who aided and comforted him placed themselves in jeopardy and at times suffered. Charges were brought by those even who by their own confession had scarcely seen his books or read them; calumnies were rehashed and revamped, nor could an earnest searcher after the truth investigate for himself because the literature was suppressed. The church leaders, from whom the persecution mainly emanated, seemed to vie with each other in reproaching, reviling, defaming, calumniating, condemning and execrating. He was called : Ketzer, Widertäuffer, Secter, Rotten-

geist, Reinengeist, Winkel-kriecher, Schleicher, Meuch-
ling, Stenckfeld, Schelmen, Ertz-ketzer, Schwärmer,
Verführer, Narren, Grillenmeister, unsinniger toller Teu-
fel, Donatisten, Valentinianer, Entychianer.

And yet in spite of it all and perchance at times on account of it all, he could not be silenced, he could not be
tempted to deny his Christ by doing an unchristian act, or
by betraying what he believed Christ had taught him by
His Spirit, the common people could not be incited against
him, many princes and nobles defended him and had it
not been for strenuous state measures, large sections of
Silesia would in all probability have adopted the " Reformation by the Middle Way." He himself labored assid-
uously in the defense of his views. He preached, wrote,
dictated to his friends, published books, and indirectly
through his adherents spread his doctrines, trusted messengers carrying messages back and forth. When the
printing presses were closed against him, loving and willing hands multiplied manuscript copies; when misrepresentations were made, he sent books, tracts and letters and
sought opportunity to explain and defend himself. When
his *Feier-Abend* drew near and the shades of night began to fall, Schwenkfeld's soul was calm, peaceful and
at rest. No undercurrent or eddy of ill-will, hatred or
revenge to others disturbed the surface and the grace of
heaven was reflected from his entire being. As all through
his life, he exemplified his life-motto: *Nil triste, Christo
recepto.* He spent his last days as he had spent a long
and useful life, in his Father's business, praying, reading,
talking about his Saviour. Fully assured that his name
was written in the Lamb's Book of Life, he committed
himself into the hands of Him whom he had served so
many years and thus fell asleep to awake in the land where
there shall be no more death, neither sorrow nor crying.

In attempting a hasty glimpse at the doctrines and motives of the man, it is well to keep in mind what he himself said of the aim and purpose of his life. In 1535 he wrote: " After God's gracious visitation some years since, I committed myself wholly to my Lord Jesus Christ and through Him in the Holy Ghost gave myself a living sacrifice into the nurture, training, and education of my heavenly Father. By His grace I do this now, praying the Lord to teach me to know Him and to strengthen and establish me in such knowledge unto the life eternal." Like the apostle whom Jesus loved, Schwenkfeld was leaning on his Master's bosom for doctrine, guidance, comfort, and, if we may judge him by his fruits according to the Saviour's rule, Jesus must have loved him. His life and theology were Johannine, Christocentric. The glory of Jesus was his master-passion: he and his followers were hence often called (perhaps partly in derision) " Confessors of the Glory of Christ." His doctrines were laid by him in earnest prayer before his Lord and compared with the Bible and the writings of the Church Fathers. Building on Jesus as his Rock and Foundation, he evolved a line of thought briefly and inadequately stated (in part) in the following propositions which are drawn from and expressed in his own words and which touch the main doctrines around which the storm chiefly seemed to center.

1. The only thing needful for man's temporal and eternal happiness, his salvation, is the spiritual knowledge of Christ, the experience of the love, wisdom and power of God in the believing heart through the Holy Ghost.

2. God is a Spirit and works man's salvation through the only mediator, Jesus Christ, the same yesterday, to-day, and forever, the Lamb of God foreordained by wisdom divine from the beginning to be the cause and ground, the

origin and end of man's salvation and not indirectly through man or the word or work of man as through channels, instruments or means of grace. Redemption and the Plan of Redemption are, therefore, the same before as after the Incarnation, with as without the historic knowledge of the Holy Scriptures or of Jesus Christ, in and through the inner, unwritten, uncreated, eternal Word of God, the Logos which was from the beginning.

3. Jesus Christ is the great mystery of godliness of whom all the Scriptures testify, the eternal, natural, only begotten Son of God the Father Almighty, the second Person in the Trinity from whom and the Father the Holy Spirit proceeds, true God and true man, undivided and indivisible as to His dual nature in time and eternity.

4. Christ's mediatorial office implies that God gives His gifts, answers prayer and receives into Heaven, only through Jesus Christ and for His sake, that the way to Heaven is through the body and blood of Christ, that He is the true throne of grace whence mercy comes, that Christ Himself is what He gives us, our redemption, our peace, our reconciliation, our sanctification, our justification, that in Christ alone can man lay off the sinful old nature and put on the holy new nature.

5. There is a duality in the nature of things which must be observed in all study of the Bible and religion. The one element is of the earth, physical, visible, pertaining to the kingdom of this world and the present life; the other is heavenly, spiritual, invisible, pertaining to the Kingdom of God and the life everlasting. The former explains, illustrates and points out the latter, but is not the latter and cannot produce the latter.

6. Jesus Christ being the Author and Finisher of man's faith, all true service derives value only from the inner,

spiritual element as the sinner hears God's Word directly from the Father and all true, public, acceptable service can and does only proceed from within outward. God is a Spirit and must be worshipped in the spirit by the heart and can not be adored by material things, services, or offerings, ceremonies or sacraments.

7. The Bible, both Old and New Testaments, inspired of God, written by holy men, profitable for doctrine, reproof, correction and instruction, though in itself dead, and without power to heal, vivify or save, and not understood by the unregenerate or the spiritually unenlightened, is, for the faithful in Christ, a treasure and mine to be prized over every earthly treasure. Its words should be read, reread, digested and meditated upon. Theology should be constructed from it and as far as possible should be expressed in its language. Faith is to be tested by it. Whatever is true, right and based upon the Word of God should be maintained and he who yields truth thus given, imperils his own salvation.

8. Sin consisting not only of the outward act, the guilt, weakness, want or defect of nature, the corrupt will or the heart purpose, but also of the total corruption, the innate uncleanness, the abiding inclination of the flesh to evil, came upon mankind through the guilt and transgression of Adam, who, after the creation, became disobedient and brought sin and death on mankind so that all are conceived in sin, born as the children of wrath and are by nature enemies of God and His grace and under condemnation.

9. Forgiveness of sin is not a mere non-imputation of sin, nor a mere remission of God's punishment for sin; it is also a killing, destroying and taking away of sin from the heart and conscience, removing all accusation and condemnation; it is a living experience and assurance of the

love, mercy, favor and grace of God in Christ Jesus, bringing peace and rest into the soul, love and joy into the outward life.

10. Man becomes a Christian and child of God when he, hearing the true Word of God, Jesus Christ in his heart, allows himself to be drawn by God the Father and through Faith to be regenerated; life, light, peace, joy, strength enter through the inner Word of God, effecting a beginning of the divine life and of the indwelling of the spirit of God. Jesus Christ is not only the mystery of faith, of the gospel and of the grace of God; he is also our example and perfect model whose footsteps are to be followed abidingly in the daily life. He who receives Jesus only as a Saviour, not as the Christian's model and ideal, has a dead Christ, a historic Christ, despising godliness and building on a fictitious faith founded on reason.

11. True Christian faith is a divine gift and power separate and distinct from all elements of earth or the works of man by which the sinner is transformed, regenerated, enlightened, and kept unto final redemption. It is not intellection, nor theorization, nor a mere conviction of the truth of the gospel or acceptance of the gospel or trust in the promise of God's mercy.

12. The true Christian Church, having Christ as its Head, is the Body of Christ, the seed of Abraham, the house of the living God, the heavenly Jerusalem, the temple of the Holy Ghost, the City of God. In such body there must be oneness of Spirit, love, faith and knowledge, and all are brethren. The visible Church based on such inner oneness should be composed of Christians, of those who call on the name of the Lord Jesus Christ and who living accordingly do not reject Him in their daily conduct. Here the Spirit of Christ rules, protects, teaches, defends

and directs all servants and services. A strict Church
discipline by which the erring are reproved and those who
live in open sin are put away from the body of believers is
an essential element in the work of the visible Church.
Outward concord in law, doctrine, ceremony or sacrament
does not constitute a Church of Christ, nor are these the
marks of a church.

13. The primary and essential element in baptism is the
inner grace of God through the pouring out of the waters
of life. The other element is the washing of the body.
Baptism of the body follows faith and is a confession of
Christ before the world, a public reception into the body
of professing believers, a visible sign of what the believer
professes to have received into his soul, a cleansing and
purification. In the Lord's Supper a dual eating and
drinking takes place — the one is invisible which the
Lord the Son of Man gives unto His own, the imperishable
bread of life which is Christ Himself through a true and
living faith; the other is visible and is called a bread of
the Lord, which the Lord has commanded to be broken
and to be eaten in remembrance of Him, by the assembled
body of believers who through faith have communion of
His body and blood. Christ did not establish the Supper
in order that the believer might seek His body and blood
in it, much less that he should seek forgiveness of sin, life
and salvation in it.

14. The Church and State, belonging to distinctly different kingdoms, should be kept separate. The State has
no right to force its subjects to adopt any particular religious services or belief, or to promote the use of the same
by force of arms, or to kill or put into exile those who
differ from the State, or to unite the sword of the spirit
with the sword of iron or in the name of the gospel to

make treaties with foreign nations, princes and powers or
to require its subjects or officers to be Christians or professors of Christ, or to build up or destroy any religious
services, or to appoint or discharge the priests or ministers
of the Church.   The Church has no right to force the conscience of any subject through the State, or to seek protection for life or doctrine under the State.

The great aims in the life of Schwenkfeld were to make
sure of the forgiveness of his sin, the regeneration of his
heart and life, the acceptance unto the life eternal by his
Christ.   He never allowed himself to become guilty of any
vice that needs glossing over, nor to speak or write a word
even to his closest friends in secret that might not be
uttered in the presence of the most refined ladies of any
period.   He was one of Nature's true noblemen who never
forgot his manners.   Through his whole life there ran a
deep undercurrent of commendable earnestness, modesty,
gentleness, friendliness, humility, reverence, playful hu-
mor, sincere piety, Christian forgiveness and a laudable
desire to be helpful to others.   The sense of the sublimity
of the character grows as one contemplates that by gently
easing his conscience, holding his theology in abeyance,
attending church once a year and partaking of the sacred
emblems at the table of the Lord, he might have enjoyed
home, peace, rest, riches, and gone to his grave laden with
the cheap honors the world bestows.

Christ having made him free, he would not allow himself to be drawn into bondage of any man or body of men
and could not be brought to pledge fealty to any church
or body of believers; neither would his genuine Christian
spirit allow him to separate himself from any godly man,
all souls being dear to him, who loved God and Jesus
Christ and lived Christian lives.   He could not and would

not play tricks with conscience; hence whatever God gave him to see he maintained, nor would he yield a jot or tittle whatever the consequences might be. This was not lack of prudence or judgment but Christ-like fidelity to truth. He loved the Catholic, the Lutheran, the Zwinglian, the Anabaptist, the adherents of all the diverse faiths, all with whom he came into contact, and, separating person from doctrine, fearlessly and freely criticised what seemed to him the ecclesiasticism, externalism, worldliness and temporizing of the churches. Criticising all, though he was not prompted by any desire for mere controversy or for lording it over others, he laid himself open to assault from all and thus became the target for many a venomous dart, but he maintained throughout a hopeful spirit and felt assured that some day his views, which indeed were not his but those of his master, would be adopted. He felt that he was in the hands of a loving Father, that even the hairs of his head were all numbered and that, though the future was unknown to him, finally redemption would be his. He as a lamb brought to the slaughter and as a sheep before her shearers never revenged himself, never returned evil for evil, never persecuted. He blessed them that cursed him, did good to them that hated him and prayed for them that despitefully used him and persecuted him.

He stood aloof from church membership—not because he did not long for Christian communion, for his big heart had a warm spot for every Christian; not because he undervalued the Scriptures, for he made it the test of all his teaching; not because he rejected the sacraments or other Christian services, for he taught that the external in worship should be observed and made use of and not be neglected; but because he could not assent to the doctrine of the " means of grace," because the patient, lowly spirit of Jesus was not observed by the churches, because the Church did not do its work in the spirit of freedom, but in the spirit of bondage; because the churches persecuted him for not believing as they did; because the church used the sword in defending and promoting Christ's Kingdom and he could not take part in it, since it is the duty of Christians to withdraw from all idolatry, error and abuse in the service of God. Less than three years before his death he wrote: "I would rather die ten deaths than join churches that on account of their statutes and articles of faith, contrary to the Bible, the example of Christ, His apostles, the first Christian churches, and the Church Fathers, burn, hang, drown, or in other ways persecute in France, Spain, Italy, Germany and elsewhere many God-fearing and pious men who accept Christ and the Apostles' Creed and live holy lives."

He never organized or tried to organize the adherents of his faith into a church. Possibly he is open to criticism on this point; but to organize meant to fight, to fight meant to betray his Christ, to betray and to confess were in his mind diametrically opposite and mutually exclusive; hence since man's salvation does not depend on the observance of any external ceremony, he did not and could not feel any call to organize a body of believers in his name. Besides, to call a body of believers by his name was in his estimation vanity and to be shunned, but when the term "Schwenkfelders" as a name for his brethren became a term of reproach he raised the question whether it was not the duty of those who believed as he did to adopt the name, lest by Satan's trickery they should be led to reject the doctrine under a semblance of rejecting a man's name.

Space will not permit any consideration of the controversies into which Schwenkfeld was drawn, or any phi-

FRONTISPIECE FROM FOLIO VOLUME OF SCHWENKFELD'S WORKS BY
THE FEIERABEND PRESS AT FRANKFURT, 1564.

losophizing on what the probable effect would have been had his spirit and attitude been assumed and exemplified in life by all those who were received into Christian fellowship or who took the name of Jesus on their lips in his and later times.   It may not be amiss to close this chapter by quoting the words of Rev. Chester D. Hartranft, D.D., Honorary President of the Hartford Theological Seminary, the most eminent and most profound living authority on the subject.   He says: " Schwenkfeld insisted on a new birth and a reformation of morals as preparatory to the reconstruction of doctrine; the restatement and development of doctrine was to be the outgrowth of a regenerated life in Christ under the Holy Ghost.   More emphasis was put upon the direct reign of the Spirit than on the formal principle of the Scriptures, though by no means to any neglect of the latter. * * * In Schwenkfeld we find the source of many characteristics of modern Protestantism; the function of the laity, the right of representation, the freedom of conscience, the separation of Church and State, the ecclesiola in ecclesia, and many another principle that is now potent in all branches of Christendom, had their strongest champion in him in the day when these were heretical principles and when their assertion was at the peril of life; there is scarcely a religious school, whether pietistic or liberal, that has not drawn some formative impulse from him through a hitherto unobserved absorption."

CHAPTER II.

The Schwenkfelders Before Their Migration to Saxony.

ℓ HE followers of Schwenkfeld were found in many parts of Germany, though mainly in Suabia and Silesia, in Italy, Switzerland, Bohemia, Moravia and Holland. In some districts almost whole villages adopted this faith. Many princes and nobles were won to the cause by the Christian life of Schwenkfeld and his disciples and by their system of doctrine, to be persuaded later to leave it again for state reasons. Had it not been for this, many others, both of the nobility and of the common people, would probably have cast their lot with the movement. In spite of the untoward circumstances, Schwenkfeld probably had at least 4,000 adherents at the time of his death.

These people were subject to adverse winds from the very first and later were practically outlawed by the Augsburg Confession, by the Truce of Nuremberg, by the Treaty of Augsburg and by the Treaty of Westphalia. In the time of persecution many embraced the provisions of law and fled to Glatz the mountainous region west of

Silesia, where more protection was afforded. At times some free city or ruling prince might tolerate them or perhaps permit them to have their own churches and ministers to be rudely robbed, persecuted or exiled again by successors.

Petitions to those in authority were suppressed by underofficers, books were burned or cast into the sea, children were by force baptized into a faith that the parents could not conscientiously accept. They were cast into dark dungeons, to waste away and perish neglected in life and death. They were placed in the front line of battle in order that they might become slayers of their fellow-men and be slain by them, but they would not shoot others, neither were they shot. They were chained to the rowers' benches on galleys to toil as rowers and then to be cast overboard when life had fled. They found their graves under the waves of the sea or by the church walls where transgressors were buried or on the village commons where offal was cast and the cattle grazed.

Their form of worship was quite simple. When they had no churches of their own, they met at the houses of the older members, sang, prayed, read the Scriptures and explained the Bible either by comments of their own or by reading the sermons of Schwenkfeld, Hiller, Werner or Weichenhan. In the training of the young they were very strict. Their Sunday services, according to one of their number, Martin John, Jr., were conducted as follows: " In the morning after each had offered his morning prayer, the people met and sang morning hymns standing, after which prayers were read from a book of prayers and hymns, particularly to the Holy Ghost, were sung standing. Song and prayer followed, after which several sermons were read. Dinner having been served, singing

Epistolar,

das ist

Missiven und Sende-Briefe

vieler hocherleuchter Creutz-Zeugen und Bekenner der
Glorien und Wahrheit Jesu Christi.

Die sie geschrieben in und ausser dem Gefängnis, an Kay-
ser, Fürsten, Bischoffe und Oberkeiten; wie auch an sich
selbst unter einander; welche alle geschrieben vom Jahre
1527. biss zum Ende des 16ten Seculi.

Darinen enthalten sind

Schöne, nützliche Lehren und Bekäntnisse ihres Glaubens
Lebens, Wandels und Gewissschafft ihrer Lehr; zusamt dem
Zustände ihrer Gefängnisse und was sie ausgestanden:

nebst einen

öffentlichen und mundlichen Gespräche, des Gott in
rührenden Mannes

Caspar Schwenckfelder,

welches Anno Domini 1535 den 28 May zu
Tübingen auffm Schloss mit Martin Butzern, im
beysein Blaurren und Martino Freisten gehalten worden ist.

Erstlich zusammen getragen
Anno 1734

und

Abgeschrieben wie auch zugleich mit nützlichen Registern da-
zugehörig versehen

M DCC XLV

COLLECTION OF LETTERS BEARING ON SCHWENKFELD HISTORY COPIED
IN PENNSYLVANIA, 1745. 972 PP., 7 X 12 INCHES.

and prayer were resumed after which reading was engaged in, to be closed by singing and prayer standing. When they met during the week, much singing was practiced and prayer was wont to be offered before they parted."

At the opening of the eighteenth century, the Schwenk-felders were reduced to less than 1,500 souls all told and were found mainly in the Silesian villages of Harpersdorf, Armenruh, Laubgrund, Hockenau, Lang-Neundorf, Hö-fel and Lauterseifen. They were honest, quiet, modest, industrious, law-abiding, and as farmers, gardeners, weavers, apothecaries, merchants and professionalists in general, earned a living — precarious indeed at times — by the toil of their hands. On account of their industry and frugality they were in general protected by their landlords. As a church they had no existence, not having at any time been allowed for state reasons to have free and undisturbed church organizations. The condition of the people at this time is described at considerable length by Balzer Hoffman, one of their number, later their pastor in Pennsylvania. Among other things he says in reference to this period of time : " We lived scattered in different villages and belonged to the church and under the ministers with respect to church service and church dues. We had no knowledge of our own system of doctrine ; indifference, lukewarmness and ignorance prevailed ; one family after another gave up the faith. Intermarriage with members of the churches took place. Those who saw the tendency hardly dared to speak on account of minister, neighbor and government. Books of new and strange doctrines were eagerly read and popular ministers listened to and the teachings of the fathers neglected. Confusion followed and he who dared to say aught against this condition was looked upon as unduly attached to Schwenkfeld and pretending to be wiser than the fathers."

The total decay and extinction of this confession of faith seemed at hand, but — as the Schwenkfelder ministers were wont to say — " God chose the persecutor's hand to transplant the faith into the soil of the New World and thus as on eagle's wings to carry it away from the land of oppression." A Lutheran minister said persecution came as a punishment from God because the Schwenkfelders did not become Lutherans. The books about the Schwenkfelders issued at this time, the conduct of Neander, Schneider and others, prepared the way for the Jesuit Mission. The immediate cause of the mission was the effort of the Lutherans to bring about the conversion of the Schwenkfelders to the Lutheran faith. Neander, the Lutheran pastor of Harpersdorf, failing in this, appealed to the magistracy. The attention of the imperial court was called to the case and there, contrary to Neander's plans, it was decided, through the machinations of the Jesuits, to make Catholics of the few remaining Schwenkfelders. Although Charles VI. did not plan to drive them from their homes, he was fully determined to tolerate only the religious parties sanctioned by the Treaty of Westphalia and thus stood ready to be led by the Jesuits. A report on these people was therefore called for and furnished in the summer of 1717 by the Catholic and the Lutheran church officers. Consultation and laying of plans followed. Judicial examinations of the Schwenkfelders were soon held. They were questioned on doctrine, their confession of faith and such books as gave light on their teaching being called for, and were then exhorted to join one of the three sanctioned religions.

The imperial government decided to entrust the conversion of these people to the Jesuits and assigned Johannes Milan and Carolus Xavier Regent to this duty. They

arrived on their field of labor in December, 1719, and by
their very coming brought consternation into the community.   They immediately went to work and at first tried
to convert the people by kind words and argumentation.
The Lutherans also went to work with renewed zeal and
tried their skill.   Rivalry thus sprang up and there was a
seeming contest between the Lutherans and Catholics to
see who could pervert the most Schwenkfelders.   The
Jesuits soon made threats against their rivals which were
not heeded.   On account of complaints, the Lutheran
ministers were then called to Liegnitz and in the presence
of the Jesuit missionaries were told that by imperial command the Schwenkfelders were to be given over to the two
missionaries, that they were to have no part in the parochial
rights of the Lutherans, that henceforth no Lutheran was
to perform any religious service for the Schwenkfelders
who were to be buried in dishonor in the carrion pit, on the
commons, or at the cross-roads or by the walls of ceme-
teries, without song or tolling of bells or train of friends
and mourners, with a wheelbarrow for their hearse.   Early
in 1721 Milan, contrary to instructions, began to compel
the women and children, instead of the grown men, to attend the missionary services.   Matters were now assum-
ing such a serious aspect that an appeal to the imperial
court was decided upon.

Accordingly, May 5, 1721, Christopher Hoffman, Balzer
Hoffman and Balzer Hoffrichter left for Vienna the imperial city as deputies to make a plea for toleration for
their severely oppressed brethren at home.   Hoffrichter
did not stay long but the other two remained over four
years.   Neither of these deputies had any knowledge of
the method of doing business at the imperial court;
officials who assisted them did so at the risk of losing their

positions; they had been grossly misrepresented; their faith was not even recognized by the Treaty of Westphalia; as a people they were hated, despised, and maligned by Church and State. Secret and true friends were found, however, in their need, by whose kind aid and counsel in part, seventeen memorials were presented to the imperial court of Charles VI. During this time Balzer Hoffman found time to write letters, visit friends, and compose hymns, sermons and extensive tracts on religious subjects. The expense incurred by the deputies must have fallen particularly heavy on a people already impoverished by the ravages of war and the burdensome fines imposed by the Jesuits. According to one account their leader Melchior Schultz confessed that to secure toleration they spent 19,000 rix-dollars ($10,000–12,500).

The condition of the Schwenkfelders at this time is well described by the Hon. C. Heydrick, in his *Historical Sketch of the Schwenkfelders*. He says: " When parents refused to present their children for instruction, they were imprisoned; women were placed in the stocks and compelled to lie in cold rooms in the winter without as much as straw under them ; and when imprisonment failed to bring the people with their children to the missionary services, fines and extortions were added; marriage was forbidden unless the parties would promise to rear their offspring in the Catholic faith, and when young people went into other countries to be married they were imprisoned for it on their return. The dead were not allowed Christian burial in their church-yards where their ancestors of the same faith slept, but were required to be interred in cattle-ways and sorrowing friends were forbidden to follow the remains of loved ones to these ignominious resting places. * * * The missionaries claimed guardianship of all orphan children of Schwenkfelders, and thus the last hours of the dying were embittered by the thought that their children must be educated in a faith that they themselves abhorred. And to prevent escape from the horrible situation in which they were placed the people were forbidden to sell their property or under any pretext to leave the country and severe penalties were denounced against any person who should assist a Schwenkfelder to escape by purchasing his property or otherwise."

The last appeal of the deputies, dated July 28, 1725, was answered by a decree from the imperial court signed "Charles" which, among the stringent regulations, contained these words: "Furthermore, the Schwenkfelder congregations in their submissive requests to be tolerated in their confession of faith in the future are once for all refused, and they shall never hereafter venture to present new supplications." This decree meant for the Schwenkfelders new terrors and for the missionaries renewed zeal and redoubled efforts to let none of their game escape. For those who were most firm in their convictions it meant flight, and accordingly plans were laid in secret for relief by this method.

The first baptism by force took place September 15, 1725, when the child of George Mentzel only three weeks old was taken away from the mother's side by dragoons, carried to the priest and baptized. The father and grandfather were imprisoned for having refused to bring the child to baptism at the priest's command. The first one to flee was widow Barbara Marckel (née Yeakel), who, with her four children, went to Friedersdorf, October 17, 1725. On the twenty-sixth of October, Adam Wiegner, in behalf of the rest, wrote to Holland and asked the Mennonites to use their influence to secure toleration and cer-

CHRISTIAN HOHBURG.

JULY 23, 1607—OCT. 29, 1675.

tain rights for them in their homes. This letter was referred to the church in Amsterdam. Investigations were instituted and while these were in progress, a second letter was written by Wiegner, December 3, in which he repeated the request for intercession in the first letter and asked whether they might be able to find a place of abiding and means of support in Holland. The oppression becoming more severe and answers from Holland being delayed, the Schwenkfelders wrote to Zinzendorf and begged him to assist them in finding a place in Herrnhut during the coming winter. The count immediately replied that in case of flight he would be glad to receive them and provide homes for them. Through a mutual friend, Pastor Schwedler, an asylum was also provided for them at Görlitz. Places of refuge having thus been located, when the storm became more severe one family after another fled during February and the following months by night, abandoning homes, and kindred and all, taking naught with them but sorrow and poverty as Adam Wiegner wrote.

Thus it came to pass that the Schwenkfelders left their homes and lands, their brothers and sisters, their fathers and mothers for Jesus' sake, to sojourn for a time in Saxony. It is irrelevant to the present undertaking to discuss the destiny of those that remained. It must suffice to say that many forsook the faith and that they did not get their full religious liberty until Frederick the Great claimed and secured Silesia and proclaimed freedom of faith to all its subjects. The handful left, though they had remained true in adversity, could not stand prosperity and gradually forsook the faith of their fathers. A century later, in 1826, the last professing Schwenkfelder, Melchior Dorn, was laid to his rest at Harpersdorf.

CHAPTER III.

THE SCHWENKFELDERS IN SAXONY AND THEIR MIGRATION TO PENNSYLVANIA.

EARLY all the Schwenkfelders exiled from Silesia found a place of refuge in Upper Lusatia, the eastern part of the electorate Saxony, ruled over during their stay by Frederick Augustus I. and his son, Frederick Augustus II. The Treaty of Westphalia defined their religious rights which of course regarded them here also as outlaws. Some were received at Herrnhut, to be transferred later to Berthelsdorf, who thus became a part of the diversified population of that celebrated community; some were received at Görlitz and a few at other places and thus between 400 and 500 Silesians gradually found homes on the soil of Saxony.

At Herrnhut, Zinzendorf seems to have given to them the right of buying land and building homes; at Görlitz they could only rent places and were not allowed to hold religious worship together in public or in private. They were in general received so well, however, that they began to think of staying permanently and made preparations accordingly. Many of them were in destitute circumstances, but they must have begun to accumulate property, for by the stories circulated and put in print one must infer that they were at least looked upon as people of means. From a reply to questions made by the Schwenkfelders about this time the following figures as to means of livelihood are gathered: spinners, 29; day-laborers, 9; carpenters, 5; dealers, 6; shoemakers, 3; linen-weavers, 3; farmers, 3; cabinet-maker, 1; tailor, 1.

They probably attended the religious services of the church at Berthelsdorf more or less regularly but they could not see their way clear to become members, for in essence it was a Lutheran body and to be received into it meant to the faithful Schwenkfelder the betrayal and surrender of many precious truths. It was probably on account of their holding aloof from joining church that they were called Silesian separatists. Zinzendorf posed as "Reformer of the Schwenkfelders," and by his course of action soon made some surmise that it would be policy for them to become church members if they wished to remain in peace, although they were not disturbed on account of doctrine or action. At Görlitz the Schwenkfelders attended the public worship of the pastor Reverend Schaeffer for a time, but after a while dropped out on account of the language concerning them used in the pulpit one Sunday.

The condition of the religious life of the Schwenkfelders was probably not as flourishing as might have been desired. They were not organized as a body and were thus deprived of the advantages of organized and well-directed pastoral labor. They were in the habit of thinking for themselves and thus did not reconcile themselves readily to the well-meant advice and directions of others. Various other things helped to thwart their religious growth.

They frequently met, however, in private gatherings at which, as well as at their family worship, the sermons of their early leaders were read and the hymns sung that the fathers used to sing. In 1732 it was reported that in Berthelsdorf the Schwenkfelders allowed their children to be baptized, but that they could not be brought to become members of the church. One of their own leaders said: " I am deeply pained when I see the pitiable decline in life and doctrine among our people." Another of their leaders said: " The heart is cold, faint, weary; zeal for the truth, spiritless and the resolution for reformation and consecration to God wanting." In view of this condition of affairs, George Weiss, one of their number, began the composition of a series of letters addressed to various members in the Schwenkfelder community. These were of a doctrinal and devotional nature and were prepared in the hope that they might be read, reread, discussed, circulated and compared with the standards of doctrine.

While they were thus living their somewhat precarious religious life, the time was drawing nigh when, under God's providence, another migration was to take place. The Jesuits, provoked by their own defeat in their efforts at mission work and by the protection afforded these people by Count Zinzendorf, had for some time in various ways engendered trouble for the Count, the Moravians and the Schwenkfelders, and were anxious to capture the game that had escaped from them by midnight flights. Accordingly when the elector died, to be succeeded by his son in 1733, the Jesuits made use of the chance afforded by applying to the young ruler for the enforced return of the Schwenkfelders to Silesia. The ministers at Dresden gave a hint of this to these people and advised them to move to some other place. An imperial edict was issued

at Dresden, April 4, 1733, addressed to the syndic at
Bautzen, the superior office of Upper Lusatia, to the effect that the *concilium abeundi* should be promulgated to
the Schwenkfelders by Zinzendorf, that they were to go
singly, and that he must see to it that the decree was carried
out.   Upon this George Weiss was appealed to and con-
sented to take charge of the religious training and instruction of the people.   Meetings were held by him on Sunday
evenings.   He read and explained hymns, and at the request of the parents catechetical instruction was also started
in connection with his other labors.   After consultation,
prayer meetings were held, at which reading, singing,
prayer and oral testimony were engaged in.   Space permits but the mere mention of the fact that the secular
training of the children was not overlooked, and that some,
like Christopher Schultz, received careful culture.

Notice having been served that migration would have to
take place within a year, the serious question arose where
to go.   The King of Prussia had made offers to them several times before the migration of 1726 to come and settle
near Berlin with the purpose of establishing linen manu-
factories, but serious objections had prevented their acceptance.   At the time of the flight they had asked the Mennonites of Holland whether they could perhaps find a place
in their neighborhood to dwell and earn a living and had
received an adverse answer.   Their friend, Hänish the
merchant of Görlitz, had advised them to try to secure,
through some mutual friend, toleration from the King of
Poland and refuge on the estates of the treasurer of the
crown, but fate seemed to be against them.   Several had
made a trip to Hamburg to spy out a place where they
might dwell together and had failed in their efforts.
Brandenburg, Isenberg, Weisenberg had been tried in

vain. They applied to the Prince of Anhalt-Cöthen, to be disappointed again. Thus they had often tried, and though at times they were almost successful, they knew not where to go.

No place seeming to be in sight in the old world, they turned their thoughts across the sea to free America, where so many of the down-trodden and oppressed had found freedom from the bonds of tyranny. Zinzendorf, who was also alarmed at this time, was looking the same way to find homes for the people under his care, the Moravians, over whom the same fate seemed to hang that had come to the Schwenkfelders. His eye rested on Georgia, which had just been carved out of the seemingly boundless expanse beyond the Atlantic, and which was planned to be a home for those fleeing from religious oppression. He proposed to them the plan of migrating in a body to Georgia.

They expressed a willingness akin to an eager desire to go there if he could arrange with the king that they should have entire liberty of conscience, free land and free transportation. In a letter to him they said: "It is not our thought to be great or to try to do great things in the world, but rather to seek to be small and to direct our purposes and settlement according to God's will. We hope to have a close connection even in temporal affairs so that our confession of faith may be upheld and that such arrangements, regulations, and conditions may be met as will enable us to win our daily bread without becoming a burden in a strange country." They were too poor to pay their own ship passage and were very solicitous to escape impending slavery and dispersion in consequence of being compelled to go as redemptioners. Zinzendorf tried to meet these conditions and entered into negotiations with the English minister in Copenhagen and the German agent

of the "Trustees for Establishing the Colony of Georgia."
According to Fresenius, Reichel, Hoffman and Schultz,
these conditions could not be met by Zinzendorf at the
proper time and thus the Schwenkfelders became free
from the hand of the count, a result planned by God for
which they had many reasons for thankfulness. The
scheme of Zinzendorf not having materialized, thoughts
turned to Pennsylvania anew, for they had known of the
place for some time already. A letter, probably written by
Zinzendorf, shows that they contemplated going to Pennsylvania by way of Hamburg before the close of 1733.
They secured permission of the crown of England to migrate to this home of the free and made preparations to
go, turning into money whatever they could. On the
thirteenth of April, 1734, but a few days before they began
to pull their tent-stakes to start on their long trip, a great
conference was held at which George Weiss read a rigorous
paper on the past and present condition of the Schwenkfelders and promulgated stringent rules and regulations for
their conduct in various relations after arriving in Pennsylvania.

The actual migration began on Tuesday, April 20, when
the first family left Berthelsdorf. In small companies
others followed, bound for Pirna, the place of embarkation
on the Elbe River. They went to Pirna in small companies because the order to migrate forbade their going in
one body, a regulation that gave them no little concern.
All having arrived by April 28, they took ship and left
Pirna on the afternoon of the following day, bound for
Altona. They passed Dresden the same day, Magdeburg on the sixth of May, and arrived at Hamburg on the
sixteenth of May. The next morning at six they disem-
barked at Altona where they remained eleven days.

They left this place in three vessels on the twenty-eighth of May and arrived in Amsterdam, the first two vessels on the fourth and the last on the sixth of June. At Haarlem they stayed fifteen days, when they left for Rotterdam, where they embarked on the ship *Saint Andrew*, Stedman, Captain, on the twenty-first of June. On the twenty-eighth of June they sailed away from Rotterdam, bound for Plymouth, England, where they arrived on the seventeenth of July. On the twenty-ninth of July they sailed from Plymouth and the next day found themselves rocking on the waves of the Atlantic Ocean. On the seventeenth of September they heard the welcome words, "Land, Land," from the lips of the watcher at the mast, and five days later the booming of cannon announced their arrival in Philadelphia.

On their voyage down the Elbe from Pirna to Altona they were crowded on the vessels, but they had the comfort of going ashore several times a day if they chose. At Magdeburg they laid in a supply of bread to last until they reached Altona, eleven days later. Quite a number of the party was sick, but no one died during this part of the journey. In Altona, Mennonite brethren, the van der Smissens, procured lodging for them and lavishly cared for all their wants during their eleven days' stay, and, after providing for their trip from Altona to Haarlem, dismissed them without taking any remuneration for their kindness and services. The three vessels on which they embarked were soon parted on account of storms and did not meet again until they came to Haarlem. Considerable alarm was felt for the belated vessels and as soon as their arrival was announced the Byuschanse brothers, their wives, Melchior Schultz, brother of the surveyor David Schultze of Pennsylvania, and other friends came out in

MEMORIES OF BYGONE DAYS.

boats to meet them and inquire about the well-being of the passengers. They found lodging in quarters provided by the Byuschanse brothers and were protected from intrusion by a guard placed before the house with instructions to admit no one except on business or by permission. The same parties made a contract with Captain Stedman for conveying the company to Pennsylvania at their own expense at the following rates: persons over fifteen years, thirty rix-dollars, persons under fifteen, fifteen rix-dollars, and children under four, free. They thrust provisions of all kinds for the voyage on them and, against their strong protest, insisted on doing these deeds of kindness, saying even to those who could pay their own passage that they should help their poorer brethren on coming to Pennsylvania. They even gave 224 rix-dollars for a poor-fund among them. The Schwenkfelders, before leaving Haarlem, prepared a detailed account of their experiences which they sent to their friends in Saxony.

When they finally embarked on the *Saint Andrew* they found that they had residents of the Palatinate as fellow-emigrants, thus swelling the number to three hundred. The voyage across the Atlantic must have been wearisome and distressing. At one time a calm would befall them so that the sails would hang motionless and the rudder was tied. At other times contrary winds took them out of their course. Storms, accompanied by lightning, overtook them, waves dashed over the vessel even up into the sails, the timbers creaked, the companion-ways and hatches were closed tight, passengers almost stifled in the hold were tossed about unable to sit or lie. The hot winds from the south and southwest oppressed them. Even their bedding was drenched by the waters of the sea that found its way through the hatches. Their food, consisting of stale

3

bread, beef, rice, syrup, pork, peas, groats and dried cod-
fish, became unpalatable and the drinking water positively
nauseating.   Nor did death leave them undisturbed; nine
times did they see their own weighted with sand or tied
to a board carried to the edge of the vessel, gently lifted
over the side and consigned to the briny deep.   Who
would not have felt like singing with them on such occasions : *Ach wie elend ist unsere Zeit*.   What a pleasure
it must have been to see their friend George Schultz — in
America since 1731 — coming over the side of the vessel
on their day of arrival, bringing with him an abundance
of apples and palatable beer.   It is pleasant to note these
words in the *Reise Beschreibung* by Christopher Schultz :
"We had a very good captain who strictly observed the
articles of contract, and very good sailors who showed
great patience with us."   Though they endured many
hardships they fared better than many other immigrants.

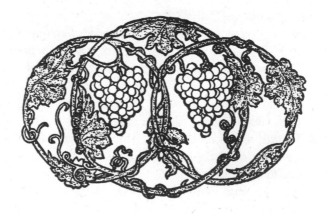

CHAPTER IV.

THE SETTLEMENT IN PENNSYLVANIA.

ENNSYLVANIA'S free soil having finally been reached, the first duty of immigrants was to proceed to the proper officers and declare their allegiance to the King of England and their fidelity to the province. Accordingly the males of these newly-arrived Schwenkfelders over sixteen years of age went early on the morning of September 23 to the Court House to meet such obligation. The minutes of the Provincial Council make this reference to the event : " At the Court House of Philadelphia, September the 12th (Old Style) 1734. Present : The Honorable, the Lieutenant Governor, The Mayor of the City and others of the Magistracy. Eighty-nine Palatines who, with their families making in all two Hundred and sixty one Persons, were imported here in the Ship Saint Andrew, John Stedman, Master, from Rotterdam but last from Plymouth as by clearance from thence, this day took and subscribed the effect of the government oaths and also the Declaration prescribed by the Order of Council of the 21st of September, 1727."

The declaration referred to reads as follows : " We Subscribers, Natives and late Inhabitants of the Palatinate upon the Rhine and places adjacent, having transported ourselves and families into this Province of Pennsylvania, a Colony subject to the crown of Great Britain in hopes and expectation of finding a retreat and peaceable settlement therein, do solemnly promise and engage that we will be faithful and bear true allegiance to his MAJESTY KING GEORGE THE SECOND and his successors, Kings of Great Britain and will be faithful to the Proprietor of this Province; And that we will demean ourselves peaceably to all His Majesties subjects and strictly observe and conform to the laws of England and of this Province, to the utmost of our power and best of our understanding."

Christopher Schultz says that they could not take the prescribed oath on account of scruples of conscience, that they were quite willingly excused from this and that they pledged their allegiance by affirmation or *mit einem Handschlage*.

On the day following, September 24, a day of thanksgiving was observed, their pastor, George Weiss taking the lead. This was the origin of Memorial Day observed each year ever since. Where this service was held does not appear to be recorded. The Court House then stood at the present Second and Market Streets. They may have met in the Friends' Meeting House close by, in one of the other churches or perchance in the woods only a short distance above Market Street. Philadelphia, then only fifty years old, had perhaps 13,000 inhabitants with farms, fields and woods reaching practically down as far as the present Vine Street, most of the 1,500 houses being south of High Street as Market was then called. Concerning this day of prayer, or *Gedächtniss-Tag* as it is commonly called, Hon. S. W. Pennypacker well says: "There were many sects which were driven to America by religious

persecutions, but of them all the Schwenkfelders are the
only one which established and since steadily maintained
a Memorial day to commemorate its deliverance and give
thanks to the Lord for it. To George Weiss belongs an
honor which cannot be accorded to John Robinson, William Penn, or George Calvert. The beautiful example set
by German was followed neither by Pilgrim or Quaker."
Here was a handful of poor and despised immigrants,
providentially saved from years of service as redemptioners
to pay their ship-passage by the charitable hearts in Holland that aided them, freed but a day from the thralldom
of centuries of cruel religious oppression, unaccustomed
to the art of church government or untrammeled public
divine services, firmly convinced that it was their duty to
maintain in their thinking and living the principles of civil
and religious liberty. Behind them was the deep sea made
memorable by a tedious voyage in deep sorrow and grief;
beyond the sea was the fatherland whose tale of ten score
years of cruelty was ineradicably engraved on memory's
tablet; before them an unknown country filled with fabled
wild beasts and cruel savages without a place of their own
on which to rest their weary heads. Their valiant endur-
ance in grievous trials is an undoubted evidence that on
the altars of their hearts the sacred fires of devotion to
their God were burning brightly and that in spite of stifling
persecution their faith in the mercy and goodness of their
Saviour had not wavered. Reverend C. Z. Weiser, in his
paper on *Casper Schwenkfeld and the Schwenkfelders*,
says: "I have often, when looking at the *Landing of the
Pilgrims*, asked myself, why some one of our Pennsylvania artists had not long ago taken the *Landing of the
Schwenkfelders* under his pencil. Such a picture would
help to perpetuate an historical event which transpired

within the career and limits of Pennsylvania, which ought not to be forgotten and over which any of the New England States would grow proud."

Before the company breaks and scatters it may be well to take a hasty glance at them. According to the list endorsed by John Stedman, the Captain of the *Saint Andrew* there are in the company 81 males and 83 females, or about 40 families of whom a dozen or more have children by their side. Tobias Hartranft brought five children; Christopher Schubert, three; Reverend Balzer Hoffman, three; George Dresher, three; Christopher Kriebel, four; Widower David Yeakel, six; Widow Regina Yeakel, five; Widow Susanna Schultz, four; Widow Susanna Wiegner, three. Other families have one or two children. There are also orphans, as for instance the three Schultz brothers. The more common family names are: Anders, Dresher, Hartranft, Heydrick, Hoffman, Kriebel, Meschter, Neuman, Reinwald, Schultz, Yeakel. Many of the children are but babes who have not yet learned to coo or to lisp the simple call to father or mother. In age, the company ranges from the helpless babe Christopher Meschter, less than four months old, to the aged Ursula Hoffman, past 71. Of the number, four have come across the mighty deep to make their last resting place in some forgotten city of the dead within the present limits of Philadelphia ere two weeks have sped away. Of the young orphans in the company, Christopher Yeakel lived until 1810, dying at the age of 91; Susanna Yeakel, until 1812, as Mrs. Abraham Wiegner, dying at the age of 83, and Rosina Yeakel, until 1820, as Mrs. Casper Seipt, dying at the age of 90.

They have in their midst a Balzer Hoffman who has stood before Charles VI., and through long and weary years pleaded for toleration for his brethren in the faith, and who has made a reputation for himself as a prolific religious writer; a George Weiss who has for years devoted himself to the spiritual interests of the flock, and is their chosen pastor to watch over their spiritual welfare in their struggles for a livelihood, and who also has won fame as a writer, an austere and fearless man of God; a Dr. Melchior Heebner, past 65, known as a successful practitioner, a Restorationist, a hearty admirer of the English visionary, Jane Leade, an outspoken enemy of false spirituality, a lover of music and poetry, a man who strongly opposed the mission of Hoffman to Vienna as a worship of the beast and a dependence on money and the aid of men; a Christopher Wiegner, who has been writing a diary of his spiritual experiences since the days of his childhood, a young man intimately acquainted with Spangenberg, Zinzendorf and many of the leading men among the Moravians, a young man whose father, Adam Wiegner, had served as secretary to the Schwenkfelders in their quest for a place of refuge and who had pleaded so strongly with the Mennonites to try to dissuade the Schwenkfelders from going to Pennsylvania; a Christopher Schultz, who as a youth of sixteen had written the glowing account of their voyage just ended, who had studied his Latin, Greek and Hebrew and gave promise of an illustrious future. In passing it will be in place to note that the immigration by Schwenkfelders began in 1731 with George Schultz, and extended to 1737.

It will be of interest to watch these people in imagination as they seek to found homes for themselves. George Schultz and his two sons David and George who like Joshua and Caleb had spied out the land, gave counsel and advice. Seemingly the father had acquired land

prior to this in Goshenhoppen and probably knew some
of the residents of the section. The son, George, afterwards known as " George Schultz of Philadelphia,
Merchant," was acquainted with the city and its ways.
These with the others that had come with them in 1733
were regarded worthy of mention by the tourist V. Beek,
June 6, 1734, when among the different sects of Pennsylvania he mentioned the " Schwenkfelders." The first
thought was to find temporary quarters until they could
look around for permanent homes. David Seipt and
family seem to have stayed in the city for awhile ; some
rented houses in Germantown or farther north ; some were
hired to people of the neighborhoods as they passed on up
towards the Goshenhoppen valley near the present East
Greenville. George Bönisch relates that early in November George Schultz asked him to come to his place in
Goshenhoppen to help on his house as mason, and that he
went there and worked for some time. Reverend Bathasar
Hoffman served as his *Handlanger* (attendant). During
his eight weeks' stay he attended services on Sunday conducted by his learned *helper* of the week. Quite a number
of Schwenkfelders must therefore have been in Upper
Hanover by November, 1734, where they probably lived
as hired people or as renters in houses erected by others
before they came.

Having found shelter and means of support for the first
winter, they toiled and looked around for places to establish themselves permanently. They had planned and
labored hard — Christopher Wiegner alone travelling hundreds of miles — to secure a large tract of contiguous
land in order that they might live close together, but
nowhere could they find a suitable place. They tried
to buy the Casper Wistar tract of over 1,000 acres in

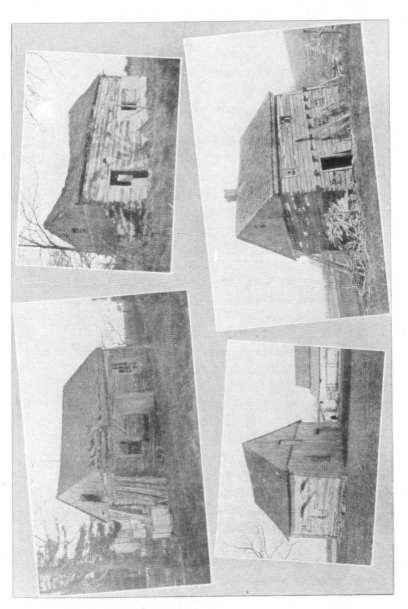

EARLY SCHWENKFELDER HOMES.

CAPTAIN BALZER HEYDRICK'S HOME, FLOURTOWN.

REINWALD COTTAGE, NEAR KULPSVILLE.

BALZER KRAUSS "PALACE," NEAR EAST GREENVILLE.

HOUSE ON FARM OF ISAAC K. KRIEBEL, NEAR MAINLAND

Lower Salford but found that it would not suit because it was already occupied in part. They made an offer of 1,000 pistoles for 2,000 acres of the Perkasie Manor lying north of the present Chalfont in Bucks County, an offer which Logan said was the best he had known to be made for land since he knew the province. Thomas Penn proposed to sell them 2,500 acres of the said manor land, but for some reason no sale was made. Christopher Wiegner relates that when he and others went to view the said land the residents would not show the boundary lines and conducted them a whole day over poor land. On inquiry, Wiegner learned that this was done because the people did not wish them to settle there. They also tried to buy 2,000 acres in "Falckner Schwam." Large unexplored and unsettled tracts were indeed available but they chose to make their homes in the inhabited sections and thus — unwittingly — avoided the extreme hardships of the frontier settlers and the barbaric cruelty of the revengeful Indian. Being prevented from establishing a distinct Schwenkfelder community, they concluded to buy wherever the conditions seemed most favorable. According to Christopher Wiegner they reached this decision March 21, 1735.

A few of these purchases will be noted. In March, Christopher Kriebel, Balzer Yeakel, father of George, Casper and George Heydrich, and George and Balzer Hoffman, severally bought lands aggregating over 500 acres situated in the present Lower Salford Township, near the Schwenkfelder Meeting House. In May, the brothers Melchior and Casper Kriebel bought respectively 189 and 130 acres in the neighborhood of the present Towamencin Meeting House. A little later Christopher Wiegner bought of Cadwallader Evans 150 acres adjoining the Kriebel tracts and shortly after moved there with his sister and mother to establish a home that became noted in its day as the meeting place of the " Associated Brethren of the Shippack," of which more will be said later on. In June, Balzer Heydrich bought of John Jacob Fauth 100 acres in Falckner Swamp, now known as Frederick Township in part, not far from Stetler's store. Doctor Melchior Heebner and his son Hans settled close by, the same year. In August, George Dresher and David Seibt bought in partnership 134 acres and Christopher Reinwald 59 acres in Towamencin, not far from where Wiegner and the Kriebels had settled. The three Schultz brothers, Melchior, George and Christopher, settled in Goshenhoppen the same year, three miles away from their uncle George Schultz, Sr. Two miles farther north Melchior Wiegner and David Meschter located themselves on 100 acres, and where Levi Krauss now lives Balzer Krauss settled on the Shoemaker tract of 200 acres. David Heebner went into Oley and rented a farm, to return later and buy land in Falckner Swamp. Abraham, Balzer and Hans Heinrich, sons of David Yeakel and Gregorius Schultz, a son-in-law, wended their way past the sources of the Perkiomen over the hills into the Macungie valley, where they established homes and acquired considerable land. A 500-acre tract belonging to Casper Wistar, the button maker of Philadelphia, was rented by them, upon which they placed Hans Heinrich and another man for the raising of horses. Abraham Yeakel and Gregorius Schultz pushed a few miles farther into the woods and secured land that was afterwards sold to the ancestor of the Fogels living in Fogelsville. While these Yeakel boys were locating in Lehigh, a brother Casper bought land in Germantown, with the idea of erecting a house and serving the community as black-smith.

In January, 1736, George Heebner entered into partnership with Henry Antes, of Frederick Township. This firm purchased 28 acres of land and erected a mill employing two sets of stone, the first mill of the community. This mill was situated where the dam of the present Grubb mill is located. It was at the house of George Heebner where the second of the Zinzendorf conferences was held a few years later.

In April George Schultz obtained a grant for 150 acres of land in Goshenhoppen west of the present East Greenville, which was transferred to the three Schultz brothers, George, Melchior and Christopher, and then, or possibly the summer before, they (according to tradition) began to build the first two-story house between the Skippack and the Blue Mountains.

In 1737, in March, Abraham Beyer, who had landed with his family in Philadelphia the previous October, bought 94 acres of land near the present Worcester Meeting House, to be joined later by Doctor Abraham Wagner who, also acquired land in the neighborhood.

In 1738, Dr. Melchior Heebner, father of George, died and was buried in Frederick Township, on his own land, according to the Genealogical Record, which he had acquired some time previous. Hans Heebner, a son, was one of the neighbors of Dr. Heebner and had acquired prior to this 94 acres.

In 1740, Melchior Wiegner acquired 75 acres of land in the lower part of Hereford Township and Christopher Krauss over 100 acres in the Hosensack valley along the creek issuing from the Powder Valley. In 1741 David Meschter acquired by patent 100 acres in Hereford Township. In 1743, Christopher Yeakel built the log cabin at the foot of Chestnut Hill known to this day as the " Yeakel cottage." In 1744 David Seipt bought 150 acres of John Benezet in the neighborhood where Casper Kriebel had settled.

In 1746, conveyances of property took place, by which the three Schultz brothers dissolved partnership. George remained at the old homestead, Melchior established himself

where Horatio K. Schultz now lives and Christopher moved to where a descendant, Jeremiah K. Schultz, lives, not far from the Washington Schwenkfelder Meeting House.

In 1749 David Schultz bought 180 acres in Goshenhoppen located near East Greenville. It was on this farm that Mrs. Schultz was cruelly murdered in June, 1750. We present herewith a fac-simile of the entry made by Schultz in his Almanac diary at the time of the murder:

In 1749 a patent was granted to Balthasar Krauss for part of the Shoemaker tract near the present Kraussdale Schwenkfelder Meeting House.   In November, 1751, Melchior Schultz bought 332 acres along the Perkiomen, south of Pennsburg down stream from the Hillegass mill property. Later in the same year, Christopher Newman bought of David Williams 225 acres in the vicinity of the present West Point.   In 1754 Christopher Wagner bought 54 acres in Worcester.   In 1757, Balzer Yeakel, of Macungie bought of Micheal Schell in the Hosensack valley 120 acres.   In November 1761 Gregorius Schultz of Macungie bought of Abraham Yeakel 125 acres in Upper Hanover, and in December Hans Heinrich Yeakel, the third and last of the Schwenkfelders who had settled beyond the present Macungie, bought the Hamilton tract of 500 acres and the usual allowance, the garden of the Hosensack valley which he later divided and sold to his four sons.   In March, 1762, Christopher Heebner bought of Frederick Cressman, 122 acres in Norriton Township and a few weeks later Christopher Dresher bought of John Roberts 129 acres in Towamencin. In 1765 George Kriebel bought of Samuel Mechling 302 acres in Lower Milford, then Northampton County, near the present so-called Kraussdale.   Later in the year, David Heebner sold his 200 acres in Frederick Township and moved to Worcester.   A few years later George Heebner, of Frederick Township, sold his farms of over 175 acres to Reverend John Philip Leidich and moved to Chestnut Hill.   These are some of the land transactions and will afford a view of the acquisition of real estate.

Through the Heintze correspondence, of which more will be said later, a request was made that the Schwenkfelders should let the friends in Germany know how and where they dwelt.   In compliance with this request, sur-

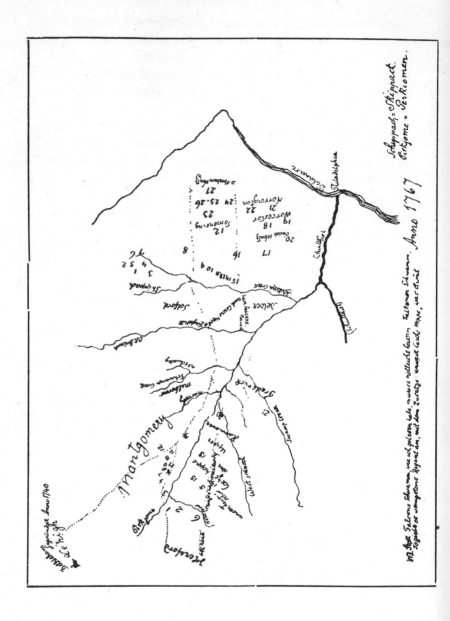

veyor David Schultze made a map of the places of residence which was sent with explanatory matter to Germany, June, 1767. When Ober-Lehrer Friedrich Schneider a century later was pursuing his studies in Schwenkfeld history he discovered this map and explanatory matter in the library of Pastor Nitschke of Harpersdorf. He made a copy which in due time came into the hands of the Berlin Library. A tracing of this copy was made under the direction of Dr. Hartranft, editor of the *Corpus Schwenk-feldianorum.* A copy of said tracing is given herewith.

The numbers on the map were explained in the letter that accompanied the map. The list is herewith reproduced in the spelling as given in the Hartranft copy on the left hand side and on the right hand side the places are identified by reference to present owners or tenants.

Berks County, Hereford:

1. Melchior Schulz.   Horatio K. Schultz.
2. David Meschter.   Leon Fetterman.
3. George Wiegner.   Solomon Schmoyer.
   Melchior Wiegners
   Sohn.
4. Barbara Jäckelinn   Joseph Yeakel.
5. Christian (?) Schulz.   Jeremiah K. Schultz.
6. Gregorius Meschter.   Not identified.

Nordhamton County, Milford Township:

7. Balthasar Jäckel, Sohn.   Benjamin Weiss.
8. Hans Jäckel, Vater.   Daniel Yeakel.
9. George Jäckel, Sohn.   Nathaniel Hiestand.
10. Jeremias Jäckel, Sohn.   Nathan Schultz.
11. Balthasar Kraus.   Levi Krauss.
12. George Kriebel.   Abraham Brey.
    Casper Kriebels Sohn.

Folgende sind alle Einwohner von Philadelphia county in Coschehoppe oder Oberhannover (translation): The following are all residents of Philadelphia county in Goshenhoppen or Upper Hanover.

13. Georg Schulz, senior.	E. H. Schultz, Palm.
14. Georg Schultz, senior alt.	Abraham Schultz.
15. Gregor Schulz.	Rufus Shuler.
16. Christoph Krause.	John C. Hancock Ice Co.
17. George Wiegner.	Late Daniel Althouse.
18. Christoph Jäckel.	Henry R. Seibert.
19. David Schulz.	Henry D. Snyder.
20. Seines Bruder. Melchiors Wittwe.	John Gerhard.
21. George Hübner.	Near Stetler's Store.

(Soweit dererste Bezirk.)

In Schippach und Umgegend wohnen; (translation): Thus far the first district; in Skippack and vicinity there dwell:

1. Christoph Kriebel.	David M. Cassel.
2. George Kriebel.	Elias Landis.
3. George Heidrich.	John Halteman.
4. Christoph Hoffmann.	Henry Derstine Estate.
5. Christoph Wiegner.	Isaac K. Kriebel.
6. Balthasar Jäckel.	Not identified.
7. Hans Jäckel.	Peter Lewis.
8. Abraham Heidrich.	Not identified.
9. Christoph Drescher.	Israel Heckler.
10. Christoph Reinwald.	Not identified.
11. George Anders.	Allen K. Kriebel.
12. Abraham Kriebel (sein Vater Casper).	Abraham Kriebel.
13. Abraham Wiegner.	Not identified.

FROM SKETCH BY RICHARDS, 1864.   YEAKEL COTTAGE, BUILT 1743, CHESTNUT HILL, PHILADELPHIA.

THE LAST LOG CABIN IN PHILADELPHIA.

14. Melchior Möschter.   Not identified.
15. Casper Seibt.   Sam Metz.
16. Hans Christoph Hübner.   William Freed.
17. Christoph Wagner.   H. H. Heebner.
18. David Hübner.   Near Worcester (Schwenkfelder meeting house).
19. Andreas Beer.   Late Michael Grater, now Ellwood Anders.
20. Abraham Anders, weiland Abrah. Wagner.   Ellwood Anders.
21. Christoph Hübner.   Wayne Heebner.
22. Abraham Jäckel.   Near Worcester (Schwenkfelder meeting house).
23. Melchior Kriebel.   Abraham H. Kriebel, "Rittenhouse farm."
24. David Kriebel der Sohn.   Not identified.
25. David Neumann sein Vater Christoph.   Jacob Heebner (?).
26. Heinrich Schneider (Tochtermann des Neumann).   Ed Wahn.
27. Melchior Wagner (von Armenruh).   Late Benjamin Wilson.

Christopher Schubert dwelt in Germantown and Christopher Yeakel and David Schubert at Chestnut Hill.

It would be interesting to trace the conveyances of land more in detail but space will not permit. In many cases the properties were transmitted from father to son or son-in-law; in some cases the larger tracts were subdivided to afford means of subsistence to the different members of the family; adjoining farms were occasionally acquired or new settlements started more or less removed from the original centers. In very few cases did the homes pass

4

into the hands of others through the financial failure or embarrassment of the owners. In a considerable number of cases the properties have remained in the hands of the *freundschafft* that originally acquired them to the present day. In each district in which they settled they found resident and non-resident land-holders who were holding the property to profit by the rise in values. The fact must not be overlooked that not all the Schwenkfelders were land-holders, that some were renters, or day-laborers or followed some particular trade.

The toil, trial and triumph of the early times form an interesting study to which scarcely more than a reference may be made. Isaac Schultz says in substance: "All the people trusted in the care and protection of the Highest as they located themselves and felt that in plodding for their daily bread in the sweat of their brows they would receive from Him the needed strength, wisdom and courage. They began at the lowest round of the ladder, to clear the land and render it tillable, and huts and houses were put up where there were none. Each by his own industry gave evidence of a hope of better times and better conditions in life. There was scarcely any relief from the toil; the burden and heat of many a day had to be borne. The bushes and wild undergrowth were cut, grubbed and uprooted. The women helped to gather and burn the underbrush, to clear a patch for gardening or for raising flax. Plows, even the primitive plows with wooden mouldboards were scarcely known, the grubbing-hoe being used instead. As harrows, bundles of branches were dragged over the virgin soil but slightly disturbed by the plying of the hoe. The uncovered seed was devoured by wild doves and turkeys in which the forests abounded. The growing grain was relished by the deer which often gave their lives as a sacrifice for their boldness in making free use of the settlers' crops, and thus became food and raiment for the white man." The women knew how to spin and they did spin. At first the spinning was not done with the familiar spinning wheel with treadle and distaff, but with a simple piece of wood that might easily be mistaken by the uninformed for a modern penholder ornamented with a ring near the one end. For the first few years they had no wool to spin because they could not properly care for the sheep. As soon as possible, however, sheep, horses and cattle were secured, bells were hung around their necks and they were turned loose and left to care for themselves in the primeval forest. Tradition says that before Abraham Moyer erected his mill on the Perkiomen where Leibert's mill now is below Palm, the people often ground their grain to meal by crushing it on stones or stumps of trees and removing the coarser and foreign elements by the use of sieves. Orchards were planted and distilleries were erected to change the luscious apple into the mischievous applejack.

The three Schultz brothers erected the first two-story dwelling house in the settlement. Melchior Neuman was the carpenter. Because they had no saw-mill, they were obliged to saw logs into boards by hand. They rolled the logs on a frame and thus devised a rude saw-mill of their own, human muscle above and below the log furnishing the motive power. Christopher Krauss also joined them about this time. They toiled at the loom as weavers and won fame by their fine linen. They manufactured looms, various household articles, wagon-wheels out of three-inch planks, horse collars out of plaited straw and traces for the harness out of hemp.

They tilled the ground. The crops which they did not need together with their finest grades of linen, some of which they sold to the governor of the Province at eight shillings per yard, were taken to market.

Balzer Anders of Towamencin and George Heydrich of Salford and David Meschter of Hereford made and repaired shoes. Christopher Yeakel and David Schubert were coopers and plied their craft at Chestnut Hill. Abraham Yeakel of Worcester, and Christopher Reinwald of Towamencin were known as weavers and David Reinwald, the son of Christopher, living in Douglass as turner. George Weiss was a weaver and for a time kept three looms going and was financially successful, often being called upon to weave for others on account of the good quality of the product of his looms. He was an honest man and made honest linen. Balzer Hoffman made his spinning wheel hum practically to the end of his eventful life. David Schultz, the surveyor, served his day and generation as surveyor and general scrivener, and as such was known favorably far and wide. Christopher Schultz, of Hereford, George Kriebel, of Lower Milford, and Melchior Wagner, of Worcester, also served their neighborhoods as scriveners. David Wagener made his way into Northampton County and established himself along the Bushkill, where he grew to be a man of means and became the progenitor of numerous descendants in Easton and elsewhere.

The Schwenkfelders occasionally became non-resident land-holders to invest their savings and thus to profit by the prospective rise in values. In case of sickness, household remedies were resorted to and the industrious housewife brought into requisition the copious collection of remedies in her well-filled bag of medicinal herbs. Should professional services be needed, their faithful friends, Dr. George DeBenneville, the Universalist, of Oley, later of

Bristol, and Dr. Abraham Wagner, of Worcester, were called upon. Accidents and misfortunes, pain, sickness and death that are wont to befall man were their lot as well, but of these there is no occasion for speaking. They toiled and triumphed in their toil. Many a father of a family could say with Jacob of old: "I am not worthy of the least of thy mercies, and of all thy truth which thou hast showed unto thy servant; for with my staff I passed over this Jordan and now I am become two bands."

They had trusted their divine Saviour, and in obedience to His sweet will, left their all for righteousness' sake and their Lord rewarded them openly in this present life. They had a practical realization of the words of the master: "Every one that hath forsaken houses or brethren, or sisters, or father, or mother, or wife, or children, or lands, for my name's sake shall receive a hundred-fold."

Thus they toiled, and in the sweat of their brow became co-workers with God in His answering their prayer: "Give us this day our daily bread." In the midst of their struggles, probably some time during 1742, the following remarkable state-paper was brought to their attention, but though they were thus highly flattered and honored by Frederick the Great, they merely acknowledged the invitation with thanks and to a man clung to their newly adopted country that they had come to love so well.

"Edict to provide for the reëstablishment of the so-called Schwenkfelders in Silesia and other provinces of his Royal Majesty; de dato Selowitz the 8 of March, 1742.

"We, Frederick, by the grace of God, King of Prussia, Margrave of Brandenburg, Arch Chamberlain, and elector of the Holy Roman Empire, etc., etc.

"Be it known to all to whom these presents may come; Whereas, we do hold nothing to be so contrary to Nature,

Reason and Principles of the Christian Religion as the forcing of the subjects' consciences and persecuting them about any erroneous doctrines which do not concern the fundamental principles of the Christian Religion. We have, therefore, most graciously resolved that the so-called Schwenkfelders, who were exiled through an imprudent zeal for Religion, to the irreparable damage of commerce and of the country be recalled into our Sovereign Duchy of Lower Silesia. We have, therefore, thought fit by these presents to assure all those who possess the said doctrine, upon our Royal word that they shall and may return safely not only into our Sovereign Duchy of Lower Silesia, but also into all our provinces, peaceably to live and trade there, since we not only do receive them into our special protection, but also will give them all necessary supplies for the promotion of their commerce. And all those who several years ago were deprived of their habitations and estates in our country of Silesia, shall be reinstated without any conpensation in case those estates are not paid for by the new possessors. Such as will settle in our villages shall have farms assigned to them, and care shall be taken to provide them employment and those who choose to live in towns shall, besides several ordinary Free years, have places assigned them gratis for the building of their houses for which purposes they need only apply to our Military and Domainen Chambers.

"We do therefore command our Superior Colleges of Justice and Finance, as well as all mediate Princes, Lords, Magistrates, etc., carefully to observe the same.

"In witness whereof we have signed this present edict with our own hand, and caused our royal seal to be affixed.

"Done at Selowitz, March 8th, 1742.

"L. S. V Cocceji.   "FREDERICK,

"per C. von Munchon."

CHAPTER V.

EFFORTS AT CHURCH ORGANIZATION, 1734–1782.

N attempting to form a conception of the religious life among the Schwenkfelders prior to the organization of 1782, the people, their leaders, their places of residence and the general religious surroundings must be taken into account.

The situation of the people themselves, considered with respect to organized religious life, was pitiable. They had been robbed of house and home, hence were poor and a fierce struggle for daily food and raiment with consequent tendency to worldliness followed; they had been deprived of Christian fellowship, hence they could not look to the old world for aid as others could and would. Prior to 1734 they had been deprived of religious liberty, hence they had not profited by the benefits of a religious organization. They were accorded no standing by the dominant religious forces, hence they probably often felt as Dr. Abraham Wagner expressed himself to Reverend Muhlenberg: "It would be no wonder if you felt an aversion from me since I bear or must bear a despised, heretical

name." Reverend Balzer Hoffman wrote: "When they
landed there was great disorder respecting homes and
means of winning a livelihood. The people lost concern
for the faith for which they had suffered and lapsed into
lukewarmness and worldliness. The whole week was
spent in a struggle for a living. Sunday meant laziness,
inactivity and a light-hearted state of mind." During the
first winter, the minds of all must have been in a state of
suspense on account of their future homes and this also
probably augmented the spiritual unrest. After homes had
been acquired and means of subsistence found, the charge
of their pastor George Weiss extended from Germantown,
possibly Philadelphia through Gwynedd, Towamencin,
Lower Salford, Upper Hanover, Hereford, Upper Milford
to Macungie in Lehigh County with spurs at Falckner
Swamp — now Frederick — and at Worcester.

George Weiss was a remarkable man.[1] At the age of
thirty-three he was chosen to write the Confession of Faith
of the Schwenkfelders and to answer the questions of the
Jesuit missionaries. In 1733 he was called upon to take
charge of the religious training of the young, probably
after notice had been served that in a year's time migration
would be enforced. In April, 1734, he wrote his *Kurtzes
Gutachten* in which he discussed the history of the
Schwenkfelders and the forming of a religious organization or Gemeinde. He also drew up stringent regulations
for the intending emigrants concerning Sunday observance,
holidays, marriage, the sacraments, prayer for children,
conduct of the daily life, etc., etc. He was a practical
apostle of the strenuous life, as is shown, for example, by
having pangs of conscience at his own worldliness in
operating three weaver's looms at one time. The worldli-

---

[1] The term " Reverend " is omitted in conformity with early custom.

SPINNING WITH THE SPINDLE.

ness of the people so vexed his righteous soul that his heart poured itself out in tears. He strove, as he said, to so live that no one could take offence at any word or work of his. His conduct, bearing and general aspect were unusually plain and simple. His whole being was charged with a holy zeal for true righteousness which he as a minister manifested without abatement unto the time of his death in 1740.

The general religious condition of the community is thus described by Muhlenberg in a letter of the period: " Atheists, Deists and Naturalists are to be found everywhere; in short, there is no sect in the world which has not followers here. You meet with persons from almost every nation in the world. The young people have grown up without instruction and without knowledge of religion and are turning into heathenism."

Beside this general inclination to a low religious life in the community which tended to counteract the labors of Weiss, there were divergent tendencies among the Schwenkfelders themselves. Dr. Abraham Wagner, of Worcester, wanted to read and did read non-Schwenkfelder books and probably affected the Beyers living close by and related. Dr. Melchior Hübner living in Frederick, was an adherent of the views of Jacob Boehme, and probably influenced those with whom he came into contact. In Goshenhoppen, Melchior and David and their father, George Schultz, and Melchior Wiegner read Jacob Boehme and Jane Leade. Christopher Wiegner, of Towamencin, also an admirer of Boehme, harbored the envoys of the Moravians, and in particular Spangenberg. The "Associated Brethren of the Skippack" met at his house and vexed the souls of earnest Schwenkfelders.

Surrounded thus and hampered by adverse circumstances, George Weiss, recognized as pastor, went to work, but he soon learned that the people could not and would not devote as much time to his ministrations as he desired, and in consequence experienced during 1735 bitter grief, dejection and discouragement. He visited various families during the summer, staying several weeks at one place, teaching the children and exercising them in catechetical questions. Some expository letters were written, but there were practically no public religious services and altogether there was not much activity. Soon after this Wiegner wrote: "My heart is often so filled with pain and sorrow in the meetings of the Schwenkfelders at their poor souls, that I cannot suppress my tears, though I speak not a word the whole time." Of Weiss he wrote: "Since we are in this country he shows such zeal and earnestness that one scarcely recognizes the earlier Weiss in him."

The contemplated marriage of two Schwenkfelders — presumably Balthasar Krauss and Susanna Hoffman — raised the question of organization. The groom came to Weiss and expressed the wish to have the ceremony performed by one of their own number. The wish was taken into consideration and as a consequence a letter was written in November, 1735, in which it was suggested to select a minister (*Vorsteher*) and two deacons (*Aeltesten*). On November 9, nine Schwenkfelders met and elected George Weiss as minister and B. H. and D. S. as deacons (Balzer Hoffman and David Seibt, in all probability), to whom they promised allegiance. A contract or agreement was drawn up and signed by the minister, the deacons and the people. This was done not as an act of union as a church, but as a means of knowing on whom the minister might depend.

Upon this Weiss assumed charge of the religious services and went faithfully and earnestly to work. Trouble

soon beset him, however. Christopher Wiegner relates
that in January, 1736, Weiss called upon him and that an
earnest discussion arose concerning a letter which Wiegner
had written.   On parting Wiegner finally promised to attend the services again.   On the following fourth of April
Spangenberg arrived at Wiegner's home, and thus added
another factor to the religious problem.   About June twentieth Wiegner made record in his diary that Weiss spoke to
them and charged them to let the Schwenkfelders alone,
saying that they could and would not agree, and that it
would be useless to try to make Moravians of them.

Without entering into further details it may be in place
to quote the following words extracted from a general
letter by Weiss, dated December 15, 1737 : "After having
tried for a considerable time the existing plan, * * * I am
compelled in protection of my own conscience to avail myself of another method to prevent if possible with respect
to myself a Gideonitish idolatry or a Jereoboamitish calf-
worship.   If you desire to use it for such purpose, I hope
before God to be excused.   My service concerning which
I have a good conscience before God, is clearly enough
expressed in the conditions of our contract or agreement
and consists of this — to reveal again and bring to light
according to my power our neglected theology.   Formal
worship is not a part of this neither is it a part of formal
worship.   For regular worship and a regular congregation
belong together.   Regular worship has indeed been established, meetings have been held, now in this place and
now in that and, though one guard against it the best way
possible, one can not prevent the growing out of it of an
established order and custom.   And it might easily happen
that at my death some fickle person with a little worldly
wisdom without savor or strength might allow himself to

be used to step into such place and in appearance to imitate the same. I, therefore, recall such ordinary regular service in my simplicity and will on my own account hold services, public and free to all. And thus I hope to place matters upon such a footing that when I die the plan may die with me." Weiss continued his labors, however, and another disturbance was soon created by Wiegner and Spangenberg of which more will be said in a subsequent chapter.

The Schwenkfelders did not stand by Weiss as they could and should have. On account of this non-responsiveness, Weiss for a time ceased going to Macungie and still later to Goshenhoppen to conduct services. Sickness came upon him and he was so depressed in spirit that he entertained the thought of giving up his public services altogether. The contract renewed in 1737 seemed to influence him, however, and he resolved to continue and thus to set an example to his flock. Later he conducted services at the house where he was staying and worshippers had to go there. The result was that many stayed away and lukewarmness grew. His feeling towards the people is probably fairly represented in these words, written by him in September, 1738: "The jealous spirits, the ignoble thoughts, the derogatory remarks, the secret envy and the idiosyncrasies both towards me as well as towards each other prove quite plainly that nothing is wanting more in you than the properties of a church" or organized body of believers.

The laxity of the people grew; his zeal grew likewise and toil followed in both districts as though matters had reached a final issue even while a weakness of body and constitution hampered him. Finally a serious sickness befell him that confined him to his bed. Full of hope that he would be enabled to resume his efforts for the young,

the unexpected summons came to him a week after he had
met his dear children in the faith for the last time in
Goshenhoppen and he was called to his reward on the
eleventh of March, 1740.

The death of Weiss left the Schwenkfelders disunited
and unorganized for religious services. His labors had
not met the success that he deserved and the people had
not reached the high ideal he had placed for them. A
glance at what he tried to accomplish must suffice. He
wished to secure a sacred observance of Sunday and the
ordained holy days by strict cessation from work and oc-
cupation of the day by reading and meditation or attendance on public worship. The married state was to be entered upon in the fear of the Lord and all worldliness and
sinful propensities were to be religiously repressed. Children were to be consecrated to the Lord and His service.
In worldly avocations men were to follow Paul's advice,
having food and raiment — therewith to be content. His
aim as to religious services is thus described by Hoffman :
" To have religious services on Sundays both forenoon and
afternoon with a kind of preparatory service on Saturday
evening, at which hymns were sung and religious exhor-
tations and explanations of scripture passages were given.
During the winter meetings were also held on Sunday
evening at which the children were catechized and instructed. On Sundays for the regular services a sermon
was read, followed by religious comments both in the forenoon and the afternoon. The three most important sacred
days of the church year were observed three days, at
which special services were held. Once a week a meeting was held in order that the hearts of the people might
be drawn away from temporal things. The children
were catechized at least two times each week and often

three times, in order that with their daily toil they might be grounded in the principles of their doctrines. Balzer Hoffman was appointed as his assistant in order that when he was away in Macungie, Goshenhoppen or elsewhere services might not be discontinued. The yearly gathering for thanksgiving, the ' *Gedächtniss Tag*' or Memorial Day was sacredly observed. When the young wished to marry they were instructed previously in Christian doctrine — particularly as to holy matrimony. At funerals religious services were also held, and soon after birth the young were consecrated to the Lord."

Upon the death of Weiss it seemed for a time as if religious services would not be resumed. An arrangement was devised that, however, was destined to be short-lived. Four heads of families (*Haus-väter*) met and agreed to hold services in their houses in the hope that the same might be introductory to some better plan. Balzer Hoffman by request took charge of the services and tried to follow the plans of Weiss as closely as possible. Dissension and discord soon became manifest again. Discouragement followed and Hoffman resigned, May, 1741. The general condition of things is shown by the fact that children did not receive half the attention they had received during the lifetime of Weiss. Hoffman was appealed to. He was touched and expressed himself in two letters dated July 9, 1741, in which he laid down thirty-six propositions to which assent was given with the result that an organization was formed again and deacons were chosen. Hoffman again resigned at the close of the church year 1744, but was persuaded to resume charge soon after. These two resignations were due to want of harmony between him and the Schwenkfelders in respect to doctrine, the daily life and views about their meetings.

In 1749 Hoffman resigned for the third time on account of health, a bodily affection making speaking and singing almost impossible.

During his ministration Hoffman had charge of the regular Sunday services, funerals and the exercises on Memorial Day. At the marriages he was occasionally asked to officiate; at other times a neighboring minister or an officer of the law was called upon. The children were trained in doctrines but not as thoroughly as in the time of Weiss; the non-conciliatory and intolerant spirit of Weiss pervaded Hoffman, and had its baneful effect, repelling men like Dr. Abraham Wagner and causing a dwindling down to less than half a dozen catechumens where there might have been scores.

After the resignation of Balzer Hoffman in 1749 a general conference was talked of but not called because many felt that under existing circumstances but little good could be accomplished. Near the close of 1753, five heads of families (*Haus-väter*) agreed to visit each other in their homes in rotation every third Sunday to edify one another and to assist one another by discussing matters of doctrine. This they chose to call *Besuch*, visit, rather than *Versammlung*, meeting, because according to their view many important things belonged to a Christian meeting which they had not undertaken. Not a word was said about discipline, or the ordering of external arrangements or the necessity of rules, or the pledging themselves together as a body. The compact thus formed was regarding only as a semi-private arrangement for religious culture by the families that took part — all who wished to attend being welcome to do so. In 1759 a few more families joined in with the services and it was decided to meet every two instead of three weeks. But the system was too limited and was far from being satisfactory. From the minutes of the general conference held in 1762, it is evident that matters seemed to be drifting to utter decay; the young people had no safe guide or direction with respect to their teaching of life, the children did not receive any catechetical instruction, there was no system for general public religious meetings, nor organization into whose hands a pious parent might entrust his children.

In view of this condition of things a general conference was held Saturday, October 9, 1762, at the house of Christopher Kriebel. The existing state among the people was discussed at some length and a paper, presented by Christopher Kriebel, was read and approved. The line of thought of said paper was that the deliverance from oppression, the replacing of the property abandoned, their preservation, the deliverance from the hands of the Indians, the blessings on their labors, the continuance of their lives should incite them to gratitude, but, to translate the wording : " We, on the contrary, have delighted ourselves in things of time; envy, slander, calumny, false accusations have separated us and the young are neglected. Such a condition of things ought to touch our hearts and cause us to tremble in view of the final judgment. We ought to turn away from these things, avoid useless disputations, live Christian lives, turn unto the Lord for direction and seek to become learners in His school. Were we to do this our yokes would be lighter and we would be reconciled to one another." A few of the lines of discussion are indicated by the following questions propounded at the conference : " (1) Will we be able to bear with one another, if a closer union is formed so that what is undertaken may not be ended in strife and works of evil? (2) Will we be willing to grant to each other the liberty of reading

SHORT QUESTIONS ON THE

THE CHRISTIAN

DOCTRINE OF FAITH,

ACCORDING TO

THE TESTIMONY OF THE

SACRED SCRIPTURES,

Answered and Confirmed.

FOR THE PURPOSE
OF INSTRUCTING YOUTH IN THE FIRST PRINCIPLES
OF RELIGION.

By the **Rev. Christopher Schultz**, Senior

TRANSLATED FROM THE ORIGINAL GERMAN
BY PROF. I. DANIEL RUPP

Skippackville, Pa.,
Printed by J. M. Schoeneinann.
1863

Kurze

Fragen

Ueber die

Christliche

Glaubens-Lehre.

Nach

Heil. Schrift-Zeugniß
beantwortet und beschhret.

Den Christlichen Glaubens-Schülern
zu einem anfänglichen Unterricht
nützlich zu gebrauchen.

Philadelphia,
Gedruckt bey Carl Cist, in der
Zweyten-strasse, 1784.

Kurze

Fragen

über die

Christliche

Glaubens-Lehre.

Nach

Heil. Schrift-Zeugniß
beantwortet und bestätiget.

Den Christlichen Glaubens-Schülern zu
einem anfänglichen Unterricht nützlich
zu gebrauchen.

Skippackville, Pa.
Gedruckt bei J. M. Schünemann.
1855

Catechismus,

Oder

Anfänglicher Unterricht

Christlicher

Glaubens-Lehre;

Allen

Christlichen Glaubens-Schülern,

Jung oder Alt,

Nöthig und Nützlich sich drin zu üben.

1 Corinth. 3: 11.
Einen andern Grund kan niemand legen, auser dem
der geleget ist, welcher ist Jesus Christus.
Ephes. 2: 20, 21.
Jesus Christus ist der Eckstein, auf welchen der
ganze Bau in einander gefüget, wächset zu einem hei-
ligen Tempel in dem HERRN.

Philadelphia,
Gedruckt bey Henrich Miller, in der
Zweyten-Strasse. 1763.

VARIOUS EDITIONS OF THE SCHULTZ CATECHISM.

authors other than those commonly accepted by us? (3) Will we be ready to bear with one another if in some point of doctrine we can not agree in our views?" The favorable answers given indicate plainly a decided departure from the position assumed by men of the type of Weiss and Hoffman. The meeting was altogether a heart-searching, prayerful and face-to-face consideration of the sad condition of affairs among them. The necessity for a closer union having been considered and plans devised, the want of a suitable catechism was also considered. Christopher Schultz was instructed to prepare his manuscript catechism for the press. The following spring it was put into the hands of the printer.

The system or plan devised was continued until the adoption of the constitution in 1782. Further details of the arrangement are given in a letter by Christopher Schultz substantially as follows: "The arrangement is that we heads of families (*Haus-väter*) jointly conduct our religious services. Each is as much and has as much right as the other, free and unrestrained. But he in whose house a meeting is held provides the materials for the forenoon exercises. He who has a word of exhortation of whatever nature, be it his own thoughts or selection from hymns or books, presents the same to the meeting upon which it is discussed and applied. For dinner we stay at the said house — except such as go to neighboring houses — and eat a piece of bread and butter according to necessity, the family always providing the guests with such meal. In the forenoon the exercises consist of singing, prayer, reading of the gospel lesson, singing of another hymn, reading of the sermon and closing with a prayer. In the afternoon we have *Kinderlehr*. Each pupil repeats a verse of the gospel lesson of the day and

VARIOUS EDITIONS OF SCHWENKFELDER HYMN-BOOKS.

all are questioned on the literal, theological and spiritual sense of the same. Catechization follows, the young being divided into classes and being treated differently according to age, etc. From this you perceive that we have not undertaken to organize a Christian denomination (*Christliche Gemeine*) to be directed and served by ministers." The meetings were held alternately at the following houses, one Sunday in the Upper District, the following Sunday in the Lower District: Casper Kriebel, Hans Christoph Heebner, Casper Seibt, George Kriebel, Christoph Hoffman, Christoph Kriebel, George Schultz, Melchior Schultz, Christoph Schultz, Christoph Krauss, Christoph Yeakel, John Yeakel, Sr., Gregorius Schultz, George Schultz. The hymn-book used by them was the *Neueingerichtetes Gesangbuch* prepared by them and printed by Christopher Saur, 1762.

Among the salient features of this period may be mentioned the following relating to organized efforts in the line of public worship. The systematic and regular catechization of the young was begun in the spring of 1763 by Christopher Schultz and Balzer Hoffman, the latter also officiating at marriages and funerals, although not taking an active part in the established system of meetings. The following year Hoffman relinquished all public services on account of the infirmities of age, being past seventy-six at that time. In 1764 the school system described in another chapter was organized and the following year the erection of a school-house at Towamencin took place, probably the first house erected for general purposes by the Schwenkfelders in America. In 1765 the justly celebrated "Heintze Correspondence" with European friends was opened. The exchange of letters with their friends since the migration grew to large proportions, and thus many personals were recorded and preserved that otherwise would have been lost. In 1769 a general marriage contract was drawn up which was renewed in fuller detail in 1779. These forms illustrate the method of procedure in case any of their young people wished to enter the married state. The latter is given in full in the Appendix. The scheme of worship and work thus devised, though a considerable advance on former plans, was in many respects defective as later experience showed.

Although the period from 1734 to 1782 may appear gloomy on account of the lack of hearty coöperation as a religious brotherhood by organizing a church or society true spiritual culture was by no means overlooked. George Weiss formed the habit of writing short religious tracts and sending them to the young under his charge. This he kept up nearly all his lifetime. Balzer Hoffman was also a voluminous writer. Catechization of the young was soon taken up and continued through this period. An earnestness of life was cultivated with which the church of to-day is unfamiliar. Much quiet meditation was engaged in, and hymns, sermons and other sacred writings were copied. Memorial Day was, during this period, the great day of the year. Weiss, Hoffman and Schultz in particular held forth on this day in powerful addresses which in many cases were copied and recopied and are worthy of being carefully studied. These addresses were mainly heart-searching, doctrinal sermons and must have had a strong influence in the moulding of their hearers.

The plan of services agreed upon in 1762 and continued twenty years threw more responsibility upon the individual worshipper, helped to develop a deeper spirituality and did not have the blighting effect of the modern system of thinking, singing, praying and worshipping by a paid proxy. Marriages were not entered into as lightly as at present. Questions were asked, a sermon was preached and the occasion made almost as solemn as that of admission to church. Marriage then was a sacred sacrament and not merely a light-hearted legal pledge or promise to be broken as lightly as entered upon. This period witnessed the formation and publication of the catechism, the *Erläuterung*, and the hymn-book, the composition of many tracts on religious subjects and of the *Glaubenslehre* in particular, the compilation and transcription of large manuscript volumes still in a good state of preservation. The Charity Fund was organized, the School Fund collected and practically all the tools devised and formed which were made use of in the closer organization that superseded this transitional stage.

CHAPTER VI.

THE ADOPTION OF THE CONSTITUTION OF 1782.

HILE considering the adoption of a constitution by the Schwenkfelders, the reader will remember that by this step the adherents of the views of Schwenkfeld entered upon a new period. Never before had a regular organization been attempted. Before 1734 this had been utterly impossible on account of state reasons beyond the control of the Schwenkfelders. After 1734 organization as a church had been resisted and thus probably prevented by Weiss and Hoffman. Of the families that migrated in 1734, only those of Melchior Kriebel, of Gwynedd and David Heebner, of Worcester, were left unbroken by death and neither of these men joined in the organization. Of the forty odd families formed in the first twenty-five years after the migration, less than a score remained and less than half a score were represented by the heads in the organization. Of those even who had joined in the organization of 1762 and had taken part thereafter in the religious services, most had passed away. The natural inference would seem to be that the original immigrants stood in the way of a more perfect union and that only after death had removed many did organization become possible. The trend of things seemed to demand the step and discussion arose and grew. A chronicler of the times says: "It is to be noted that about the year 1781 a movement began to manifest itself more and more among our people to unite themselves more closely into a religious society, in order that in a mutual way such regulations and arrangements might be made and agreed upon among ourselves as would be serviceable to good conduct and edification and the upholding of our Christian confession of faith and the maintaining of a proper discipline. Many were indifferent, mutual mistrust seemed to fill some hearts and there was so much lukewarmness manifest that utter ruin seemed to stare the people in the face. There was great neglect in the fulfillment of ordinary Christian duties. The children were remiss in Christian culture, the young people upon and after marriage showed scant attention to the doctrines of the fathers, many seemed to be surcharged with envy and calumny and indifference concerning many serious matters prevailed."

In the movement Christopher Schultz was the leading spirit and well earned the name "Father" in this connection. Others, indeed, took important parts and should not be forgotten, but he preëminently deserves to be recognized for the leading place he filled. In the deliberations frequent reference was made to the writings of Schwenkfeld, Christopher Schultz and a recently published tract on church discipline issued by the Quakers, the duty of Christian fellowship was strongly advocated and the question raised how any one could have a right to separate himself from others.

At the first constitutional convention held in the "Lower District," February 5, 1782, the condition of the Schwenk-

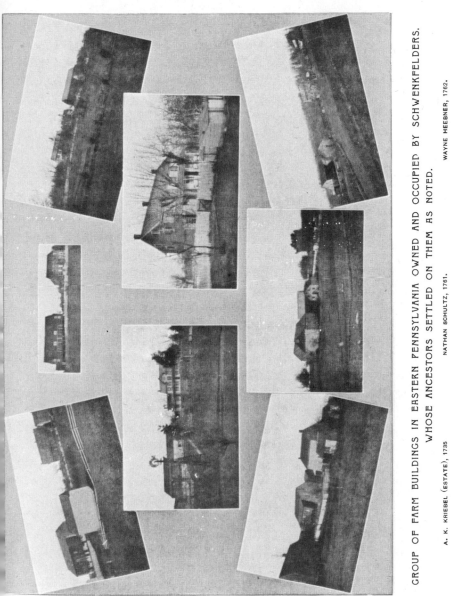

GROUP OF FARM BUILDINGS IN EASTERN PENNSYLVANIA OWNED AND OCCUPIED BY SCHWENKFELDERS.
WHOSE ANCESTORS SETTLED ON THEM AS NOTED.

A. K. KRIEBEL (ESTATE), 1735   NATHAN SCHULTZ, 1761.   WAYNE HEEBNER, 1762.

H. H. HEEBNER, 1754.   ISAAC K. KRIEBEL.

LEVI KRAUSS, 1735.   JEREMIAH K. SCHULTZ, 1743.   ABRAHAM SCHULTZ, 1735.

felders and their children was considered, some remarks were made and the following questions proposed for consideration: "(1) Is it necessary and profitable to educate children in Christian doctrine? (2) Can more time than formerly be allowed for their instruction? (3) Should a different method or other teachers be employed in teaching? (4) Should not the newly married devote more time to the study of Christian doctrine?" At the second conference held in "Coshehoppe," a rough sketch of the contemplated constitution was discussed. The third conference was held in Towamencin, June 1, 1782. After some preliminary discussion the proposed constitution as drawn up by Reverend Christopher Schultz was laid before the meeting under the name: "*Vorschlag nützlicher Stükke bey einer religiösen Gesellschafft in christliches Bedeneken zu Ziehen.*" Some at once gave their assent to the scheme and others asked time for consideration. The questions raised at the first conference were then discussed. The first was answered in the affirmative, the second was laid on the table, the third was answered in the negative, and the fourth was laid on the table. It was agreed that all who gave their assent to the proposed constitution should sign it in testimony thereof. The following form of subscription, as adopted August 15, was annexed to the constitution and then signed: "We, the undersigned, hereby declare in writing, that we approve the above constitution and that it is our desire that our society may be united on said plan, and each of us hereby promises that by the help of God he will in his weakness help to promote the same." George Kriebel said on Memorial Day, 1789, that Christopher Schultz told him that the constitution was given as he first wrote it without changing a word and that he felt a movement in his heart as the same was put into his mind.

The Constitution or Fundamental Principles of the Schwenkfelder Church, as Adopted in 1782.

1. Every person desiring to be a member of this Church should concern himself about a proper and approved ideal upon which the members are to be established in all things, and in accordance with which they are to form their union.

2. All those who would be in this religious association should place this foundation and ideal before their eyes as an aim set before them for which they are to strive with becoming zeal and energy.

3. In God's nature one beholds love primarily as that excellent outflowing virture which binds together God and man. All those who wish to take sure steps for the realization of said ideal must, first of all, form and maintain their unity by this bond of perfection among themselves.

4. Built on this fundamental principle of the divine nature — namely, love — their single, immovable aim must and will be to glorify God and promote the general welfare of each member.

5. In compliance with such object, their first care in their common affairs must be directed to a proper arrangement of public worship flowing from said foundation and agreeing with said ideal.

6. The gospel or word of God is the treasure which the Lord Jesus gave his apostles, and by which, as He commanded, the nations were to be called to faith and gathered, to be nurtured and ruled. It is the chief element in public worship and the rule of all its exercises.

7. It follows that they not only ought to possess this treasure, but they must also, with care, see to it that the gospel and the word of God are preserved and practiced by them in purity and simplicity, without which they cannot be nor remain a Christian people.

8. It follows, also, that they must have persons among themselves who know, live and teach the doctrine : otherwise it would be a dead letter, and could not bring about the good referred to in 6; hence proper plans must be devised in this respect.

9. There follow also the unceasing effort and care for the instruction of youth, both in what may be learned in schools as also in what should be taught in the study of the word of God or Christian doctrine, without which their aim referred to in 4 cannot be maintained nor the doctrine be upheld.

10. The repeated voluntary gathering for public worship with appointment of time and place for the same belongs also to the common care and concern.

11. Besides the appointment of public worship and the practice of God's word, a religious society, if it would at all attain its object, must strive to uphold a proper discipline among themselves, in order that through the same a guard and restraint may be set against the attacks and hindrances of the evil one, and that his work may be destroyed where it has taken root; that a good and useful deportment may be maintained in intercourse and conduct; that the hand of mutual help may be offered under all occurrences, and that virtue and good morals may be promoted.

12. They must have fixed rules and regulations among themselves by which they may know who belong to their society or not; they must also use diligence to keep correct records of all that is enacted by them and upon which they have mutually agreed in matters relating to discipline, in order that no one may take ignorance as an excuse, but that all may conform thereto.

13. Since good rules are necessary in the exercise of commendable discipline, the revealed will of God con-

tained in the Ten Commandments in their full and perfect sense will be to them the best and most adequate rule for the promotion of good conduct or morals, for defense against the evil, for discriminating between the good and the evil.

14. In conformity to their aim and rules, they will, besides this, also consider useful and proper regulations, so that commendable decorum may be preserved under the diverse circumstances, as marriage, training of children, family life, death, burials and the like.

15. The practice and maintenance of such discipline and regulations will always have their temptations, since we all carry these by nature in our own bosoms; it will, therefore, likewise be necessary to have faithful persons who will see to it that discipline and good order are not neglected, but maintained and promoted by each member.

16. In order, however, that such service may not be made too difficult, but be possible and endurable for such persons, each and every member, by proper regulations, must take part in said exercises and supervision, whereby at the first notice of the outbreak of an offence its progress may at once be checked, and the deacon not be troubled by it.

17. Certain conferences should also be appointed as time may occasion or the circumstances of the general welfare may demand, at which the condition of the Church, for weal or woe, may be considered, doubtful or questionable matters decided, and the general welfare and useful arrangements and institutions in general may be cared for.

The following were the original subscribers to the constitution: George Schultz, Christopher Yeakel, Christopher Schultz, Jacob Yeakel, David Schultz, Christopher Krauss, George Wiegner, Abraham Schultz, Balthasar

Schultz, Andrew Schultz, George Kriebel, Jeremiah Kriebel, David Schultz, Melchior Schultz, Balthasar Krauss, Christopher Meschter, Casper Yeakel, Christopher Schultz, Jr., Melchior Yeakel, Balthasar Schultz, Gregorius Schultz, Matthias Gerhard, Christopher Hoffman, Abraham Kriebel, Melchior Kriebel, Jr., Jeremiah Kriebel, Christopher Schultz, Abraham Kriebel, Jr., Andrew Kriebel, George Kriebel, Jr., George Heydrich, Abraham Drescher, George Heebner, Melchior Schultz, Jr., Christopher Yeakel, Jr., David Kriebel, Christopher Yeakel, Abraham Yeakel, Peter Gerhard, George Anders, George Schneider.

These 41 organizers are called *Haus-väter* (House fathers, heads of families) and a study of the names shows that in all probability they were all married men. The widows and the wives, the unmarried young men and young women are thus made conspicuous by their absence. That they were not overlooked will be shown in another connection.

On the 23d of September a conference was held at which, among other proceedings, the following explanation was recorded; that the aim of organization into a religious body is not to set a net to be drawn tight after persons are caught, nor to make contracts that children must be put under religious instruction a certain length of time as some might suppose, but to show that the duty towards Him and our fellow-men placed upon us by God is recognized and that an effort will be made mutually to help each other to fulfill the same.

It may not be amiss in conclusion to quote the following words of Christopher Schultz penned on the occasion of the completion of the constitution. He wrote these words:

"It is indeed easy to place a proposition on paper and perhaps even to give consent to it. The proper grounding of the same within one's self and its carrying out are a different matter. The former without the latter is but vanity, however good and necessary this may be. It is incontestible that if such a plan is to be carried out, love must have its due place and must rule within us and between us. Wherefore we must needs be concerned about this foundation and seek after it, in order that it may manifest itself in us from all sides, so that its work and fruits may give evidence that we are Christ's disciples. The most serious question, indeed, with me is, whether at this time such a plan can continue to exist among us. Let us not flatter ourselves. For this purpose it is necessary that we place plainly before our minds the nature and marks of love as described by the Apostle Paul, and then that we look back upon ourselves to see how far these marks have shown themselves within us. The Lord tells us that he who would build a tower should first sit down and count the cost whether he have sufficient to finish it; otherwise he might as well leave it undone. He who tries to follow this counsel will here find occasion to be seriously afraid and concerned with me in consideration of the sorrowful product that manifests itself in mutual conduct and inclination. I confess that although in the projecting of the *Vorschlag*, I was favorably inclined and, as it were, led in a becoming ease of mind, certain things came up to my mind soon after that depressed me considerably. Meanwhile, giving up is a most sinful despair while God lives. Whatever weakness and shortcoming may be in us, in Him is and may be found full counsel and compensation but we do not concern ourselves about the affliction of Joseph and sleep on beds of ivory. In the name and by the command of our faithful mediator and intercessor let us press in and besiege the throne of grace. How welcome, indeed, would we be before our holy Father in heaven, were we to implore Him for the proper thing, the gift of His love! O! my beloved! we must make up our minds to this, otherwise all our toil will be useless. We must also implore Him for the pardon of all that we have hitherto done against His love. It is also necessary that we learn to recognize and to admit our duty and show our consequent inclination heartily to pardon one another. Effect this within us all by thy Spirit, O, Father of all grace, for the merits of thy dear Son, to thine own eternal glory, Amen."

CHAPTER VII.

CHURCH LIFE UNDER THE CONSTITUTION OF 1782.

LL the various activities pertaining to church life conducted by the Schwenkfelders at the adoption of the constitution were of course continued and assumed by the new organization subject to the proper limiting conditions. The relation of this body to the teachings of Schwenkfeld are thus expressed by the *Formula of Government*: "The members of the Schwenkfelder church believe that the Bible is the sufficient and only infallible rule of faith and practice and in their interpretation of the same follow for substance of teaching the system of doctrine as taught by Casper Schwenkfeld of Ossig." The constitution as adopted and referred to in the previous chapter was frequently copied and thus circulated. It was first printed as an appendix to the *Erläuterung* of 1830 and became a part of the *Constitution and By-Laws of the Schwenkfelder Society*, issued in 1851, of which an English version appeared in 1882 and revised editions in 1898 and 1902, known as the *Formula for the Government and Discipline of the*

(80)

SCHWENKFELDER MEETING HOUSES IN PENNSYLVANIA.

TOWMAENCIN, 1893.
HOSENSACK, 1838-1893.
WORCESTER, 1836.
WASHINGTON, 1824-1883.
PHILADELPHIA, 1898.
WORCESTER, 1882.
SALFORD, 1869.
KRAUSBDALE, 1857.

Schwenkfelder Church. These various editions were growths and evolutions of the scheme as mapped out in 1782, adapted to the needs, wants and emergencies as they manifested themselves. The term "Church," as applied to this body of believers is of quite recent date, the earlier terms being Gemeinde, Gemeine, Gesellschafft, Society, Fraternity. The term "Schwenkfelder" is used in preference to "Schwenkfeldian" because it is the customary word in all records of the past and in legal papers of the present.

Christopher Schultz, by request, drew up an "Appeal" to the young in 1783, to encourage them to join the "Society." It was also agreed that in the case of women signing should not be called for at their admission, a mere word of assent being considered sufficient. The questions asked at the admission of members were used quite early in the history of the organization, but the authorship of the same seems to be forgotten, tradition pointing however at George Kriebel.

Christopher Schultz's "Appeal" was used frequently in entreating the young for membership, but with all this the spirit of freedom was so strong that the winning of new members was not an easy task. The records show that as early as the year 1803 there was a period of great laxity in church matters; many had wandered away to other churches, the parents were indifferent about their children and affairs in general were at a low ebb. Parents were urged by resolution to use proper efforts to encourage their children to join the society and members pledged themselves anew to use diligence to promote the welfare of the body. In cases of discipline names of offenders were omitted from the minutes and an effort was made to win back those who for any reason had severed their connec-

6

tion with the society. During this period many of the young people neglected to join the church until they expected to be married, when the rules and regulations made membership a necessity if they hoped to have the ceremony performed by a minister of the society.

By resolution it was agreed in 1828, at a conference that children over whom the prayer for children had been pronounced should be considered members of the society. This rule was a dead letter and is not regarded at all by present regulations. At various periods defections took place to other religious bodies. Joshua Schultz said : "It has never been the custom of these people to make proselytes; on the contrary, they were content when they were not assailed by others on this account. However, notwithstanding their endeavor to conduct themselves as the *Stille im Land* and attend to their own calling, they did not escape these troubles." For the last twenty-five years the church has enjoyed a more earnest effort to win membership and the cold indifference has been replaced by a more becoming zeal.

Meeting Houses.— The first place for public worship owned by the Schwenkfelders in America was erected of logs in the summer of 1790 where the present Hosensack meeting house now stands. At one end a school-room was partitioned off, supplied with tables and benches, where for many years a parochial school was conducted. The first services in this building were held August 8, 1790, the tenth Sunday after Trinity. This log building was replaced by a more modern though plain and unpretentious stone structure in 1838 which a noted minister was accustomed to call a mill. It was remodelled in 1893. The second meeting house was erected in 1791 where the present Washington Meeting House stands. The first services at this place were held on Memorial Day, Saturday, September 24, 1791. In 1824 it was proposed to build a new and more modern house of worship. Neither the vigorous resistance of David Schultz against the sacrilegious destruction of the old building nor the plea of others to build the new house at a place near the present Palm Station so as to have only one place of worship prevailed and the new building went up the same year. It was remodelled in 1883.

The first meeting house in the so-called Lower District was erected in 1793 where the present Towamencin meeting house stands. The school-house that stood there and had done service for many years, probably gave way for this new structure. The first services were held July 21, 1793, the eighth Sunday after Trinity. According to Edward Mathews: "This building was of logs, pebble-dashed, with the gable ends weather-boarded and painted red. There was a portico in front with seats on either side. The date over the portico was of 1795 (3 ?)." This building was replaced in 1854 by a plain stone structure which in turn gave way to the present brick building in 1893. In 1825 the first Kraussdale meeting house was built which did service until 1857 when it was replaced by the present brick building which was remodelled in 1900.

The present meeting house at Lower Salford, the first at that place, was erected in 1869. At these five places of meeting, school children were taught in the week during the winter months practically up to the adoption of the public school system. In 1835 the question was raised whether it would not be advisable to erect a house of worship in the Worcester district. The result was that the following year a meeting house was erected where the Worcester meeting house now stands. This was re-

placed by the present, more modern building in 1882.
It is worthy of note that the latter building was the first one
to have a basement for Sunday-school purposes erected
by the Schwenkfelders and that this innovation met with
considerable vigorous opposition.   When the Towamencin
meeting house of 1893 was built, the basement was regarded a desirable improvement and no opposition was
encountered.   The first Mission church building was that
of the First Schwenkfelder Church in Philadelphia, Pa.,
and was dedicated October 23, 1898.

The Ministry.— At the time of organization, brethren
were elected to whom the customary ministerial duties
were entrusted.   This action did not imply the creation of
a priestly class or a recognition of a division of the membership into clergy and laity.   Duties were then not as
exacting nor the services as frequent as now ; men were
chosen who had been brought up in the atmosphere of the
teachings of the Schwenkfelders and had thus been indoc-
trinated quite thoroughly.   No fixed salaries were paid —
in fact practically no financial remuneration was given,
though the ministers were not allowed to live in want.
Although no distinct previous resolution had been passed
when the first edition of the *Constitution and By-Laws*
was adopted in 1851, a clause was inserted in the By-Laws
saying that the minister was to perform his services gratis,
quoting (or rather misquoting) Christ's word, "Freely ye
have received, freely give," specifying, however, that the
ministers were to be excused and exempted from all out-
lays which occur in the church and which may be called
church expenses.   This was not in harmony with the
teaching of the *Glaubenslehre* adopted half a century
before by the Schwenkfelders saying that it is a duty of
hearers towards the preachers, "*Sie nach Nothdurfft zu*

versorgen." As years rolled on and the changes incident to the life of the community manifested themselves a different view began to prevail as embodied in the *Formula of Government*, 1898. With no prospect of any financial remuneration, young men could scarcely be expected to take a full course of theological training as is the present custom the youngest ministers, Rev. O. S. Kriebel, being a graduate of Oberlin University and Theological Seminary, and Rev. E. E. S. Johnson, of Princeton University and the Hartford Theological Seminary. The ministers were elected by the male members of the church by ballot and were expected to assume duty at once. They served for a period of several years as " Licentiates," or " *Lehr-Candidaten*," before they were made full ministers. The average of the ages of these candidates at their final election from first to last is 44 years. Good results were obtained, but it would be rash to say that the best possible results can be obtained by such methods. On account of the rural type of membership the ministers were in nearly every case farmers who followed such worldly vocation in connection with their pastoral duties.

Though these servants of God had not studied in the theological schools and did not receive pay in dollars and dimes for their labors it would be unjust to think of them as weak, unlearned, unsuccessful preachers. Reverend John Schultz (1772–1827), who had been brought up under these circumstances and who, while toiling as a farmer, served his church very acceptably as a minister, in transmitting a sketch of the Schwenkfelders, wrote a letter to Pastor Plitt, of Philadelphia, 1820, that called forth these words : " This letter seems to be filled with such a spirit of love and moderation that John the beloved disciple might accept it as his own. In orthography and the simple but strong and pure old German style, the writer surpasses many of our present young ministers. We are told that this man, although a farmer, has devoted considerable attention to theological knowledge and has attended a Latin school."[1] Of Christopher Schultz, Jr. (1777–1853), Rev. C. Z. Weiser had this to say : " Tall, venerable, talented, self-educated and pious, he won their esteem and love as well as the good-will of the surrounding Church membership.* * * Through him more especially, had the intercourse and fellowship with the Reformed and Lutheran congregations become intimate. At well-nigh every funeral occasion, the Schwenkfelder pastor Schultz was invited to officiate at the house of mourning. So far indeed had he gradually and quietly ingratiated himself into the love and esteem of the Reformed congregations especially that during a vacancy occurring in the history of one of the latter, through the pastor's death it was seriously proposed to employ Pastor Schultz as a supply until a pastor of their own should be elected."[2]

The Diaconate. — According to the constitutional provision, at a conference held November 11, 1782, it was agreed to elect four deacons, two for each district, and a committee was appointed to draw up regulations for said office. At the next conference the following report of the committee was adopted : "(1) In each district two persons shall be elected as deacons. (2) The main rule for the guidance of the deacons shall be the ten commandments. (3) Attention must be paid by said deacons to all classes, the young and the old, alike. (4) In case of complaint by members, the deacons must see that the complainants themselves fulfill their duties. (5) They are

[1] Hosensack Academy.
[2] *Mercersburg Review*, July, 1870.

not to give judgment in any case until they have heard
both sides of the case. (6) The deacons are to be no
respecters of persons. (7) Offenses of a private nature
should be adjusted as quietly as possible.

At the fall conference, 1798, it was agreed that three
deacons instead of two, should be elected for each district
and that the oldest in office should be ineligible for one year.
The latter provision was cancelled in 1803. The expected
happened and the burden of the work was thrown upon a
few members who were reëlected from year to year. On
account of the frequent reëlection of the same officers, a
rule was adopted in 1857 by which a deacon could not be
his own successor. The spirit of the rule was carried still
farther by a resolution of 1888 according to which a
deacon at the close of his term of office is ineligible for
three years. The deacons are the regular channels for attending to the temporal affairs of the church, and are set
as watchers to keep guard over the lives of the members.

Incorporation. — The school trustees held the property
used by the Schwenkfelders in the furtherance of their
educational enterprise and naturally became the custodians
of the property when they began to build houses of worship. When in 1838 the Flinn will contest was forced on
the Society or more particularly on the " Charity Fund,"
the argument was used that no such body as the " Society
of Schwenkfelders " legally existed and that therefore all
bequests to the said fund were null and void. The defense was that such society had existed for a hundred
years and that they were well known and the only body
known by that name. To remedy the defect and insure a
legal holding and transferring of property, the trustees and
treasurers of the Charity and the Literary Funds were incorporated under the style and title of " The Managers of

the Literary and Charitable Funds of the Society of
Schwenkfelders." The exigencies connected with mission
work developed a necessity of amending the said charter which was accordingly done in 1897 with the purpose
of adapting it to the changed conditions and requirements.

The Charity Fund. — The Schwenkfelders came to this
country poor and had to struggle for a living but they never
allowed those to suffer with whom they were thrown in
church relationship. The raising of money to help a
needy brother in 1768 occasioned the founding of the
Charity Fund in 1774. The caring for the poor, the suf-
fering and the unfortunate being naturally one of the
duties of a Christian church, the fund was appropriately
assumed by the society at its organization. In defining
the scope of the fund in 1789, it was agreed that the fund
was to be devoted to the alleviation of the condition of the
poor and to other worthy causes. In the year 1790 each
district began to elect its own treasurer of the fund and
this has been the case since. In the spring conference,
1815, it was agreed that aid might and should be given to
the poor even if not connected with the society. Ed-
mund Flinn, who died in 1836, bequeathed a portion of
his estate to the fund. The will being contested, litigation
followed. A charter was secured as stated above; the
will was sustained and in 1845 the fund finally received
the bequest. In 1855 it was agreed to give money out of
the fund to the ministers to be distributed as they saw
fit among the poor by way of charity. This regulation
happily did not become a custom. By resolution it was
later agreed to pay out of the Charity Fund the bills
for medical attendance on ministers and the expenses incurred in repairing church buildings. The scope of the
fund was widened still further by the resolution of 1890

GROUP OF SCHWENKFELDER MINISTERS.

JOSHUA SCHULTZ.	JOHN B. KRIEBEL.	GEORGE K. MESCHTER.
1808-1892.	1841-1882.	
JACOB MESCHTER.	REUBEN KRIEBEL.	EDWIN S. ANDERS.
1818-1891.	1820-1890.	
	WILLIAM S. ANDERS.	
GEORGE MESCHTER.		E. E. S. JOHNSON.
1808-1887.	O. S. KRIEBEL.	

according to which the deacons have the right to appropriate the unexpended interest each year for general church purposes. The fund was raised by Sabbath collections, bequests, thank offerings, interest, sale of books, donations, etc.

Board of Publication. — This board was created at the adoption of the *Formula of Government* and sprang out of the committee for the publication of the *Corpus Schwenkfeldianorum.* Prior to this the publication of books was attended to by special committees appointed for such purpose. A few publications were issued by private enterprise, and later assumed by the society.

Missions. — In mission work the Schwenkfelders as a body have proportionately not accomplished the amount of work done by other religious societies. Poverty, location and the treatment received at the hands of others may in part account for this. Neither have they heralded their deeds abroad nor received credit for what they did through various other denominational channels. As a body they raised money for Bible societies, tract societies, educational purposes and mission boards irrespective of sectarian lines. As individuals they gave succor to many a worthy cause without letting the one hand know what the other was doing. By the incorporation of the Mission Board, renewed impetus was given to mission labors, and a channel afforded by which the gifts of members to such cause may receive proper credit and the whole effort be systematized. Though only called into existence as late as 1895, the board has already become the arm for reaching out and building up the First Schwenkfelder Church of Philadelphia, the first mission of the church, organized December, 1898. It is also conducting work in China, India and Armenia.

Literary Fund. — The system of schools inaugurated in 1764 became a part of the work of the Society. The school plan will be considered in a subsequent chapter (Chapter IX.). By conference action 1823, the system was placed directly in the hands of the society, all members being eligible as trustees and having the right of voting. The fund was thereafter devoted to the repairing of the school-houses, the education of poor children and other benevolent purposes. As thus reorganized the fund has been known in later years as the Literary Fund devoted mainly to the publication of books and tracts.

Secret Societies. — In reference to secret societies, it may be in place to remark that the whole trend of the life and doctrine of the Schwenkfelder faith is opposed to the very idea and spirit of secresy, to the taking of all oaths, to the unchristian rules regulating their membership and administration of funds. At the fall conference, 1820, in conformity with the spirit of the times then prevalent the question was raised "whether, on account of the continued spread of the so-called order of Free-Masons, it is not necessary to indicate the sense of the society in reference to such societies for the sake of our members and our children." The following resolution was accordingly adopted: "Since the order of Free-Masons is clothed in mystery and in many dark, typical and curious customs and much that is offensive is presented in their processions and in the bearing of their members, and since we are directed by the Bible and the writings of the Fathers away from sin to our salvation and Saviour, Jesus Christ, we must in the highest degree disapprove their course if any of our members bind themselves by oaths to such orders, and their course must be regarded as impertinent behavior and we would herewith exhort all to keep aloof from the same and on the contrary abide by Paul's word, 'mind not high things, but condescend to men of low estate.'" In 1851 the following was adopted: " Resolved, further, that it is contrary to and against the doctrine and confession of this church that any member should connect himself with any such order or with any secret society as, for example, the Order of Free-Masons, Odd Fellows and the like." After considerable discussion the General Conference of 1897 agreed on a statement embodying the earlier position and giving more explicit reasons for the same.

Marriage Regulations. — The following regulations relating to marriage were adopted at the fall conference, 1783. (1) The contracting parties must both be of our own confession. (2) The consent of parents or guardians on both sides must be secured. (3) The groom is to announce his intentions to one of the ministers, who is to inquire whether conditions one and two have been complied with, whether both have become members of the society, and whether they are willing to help to advance the interests of the society. Ministers have the right to refer the groom to the deacon and he to the society if the answers are not satisfactory. (4) Such persons are to be instructed in Christian doctrine. (5) Bans shall be published. It was also resolved that in case the bride did not belong to the society the groom was to try to persuade her to become a member, and if she did not, the ministers were not to perform the marriage ceremony. The following year, at the request of the society, Christopher Schultz drew up a form of betrothal that might be recommended to the young. The society was opposed to the intermarriage of those who are closely related and at various times had occasion to take up cases for consideration where the young failed to keep this in mind. The rules and customs relating to marriage and admission of members so frequently led the young to put off the joining of church until they expected to be joined in marriage that the matter on several occasions became the subject of discussion in general conferences. In 1827 the following resolution was adopted: "When a person or persons of our confession or members of our society have been married by ministers not of our society and have afterward expressed sorrow for such step to a minister or deacon, it shall become the duty of the ministers to ask such party in public meeting whether he is still sorry for such step, and if a satisfactory answer is received such party shall not be excluded from membership." In 1851 the question of "mixed marriages" was again raised and it was resolved that, according to the doctrines maintained by the society, both parties ought to belong to the same faith. In 1866 it was agreed to permit the performance of the marriage ceremony by ministers without publishing the bans, if one or both parties did not belong to the society, but to require the same in all other cases. The custom became a dead letter without conference action about the year 1877. The restrictions and regulations thus imposed at various times were gradually moderated or abandoned, so that many became a dead letter long before the revision of 1897.

Church Discipline. —The very object of the organization included the idea of discipline and the members would have been grossly derelict in their professed purposes as a society if they had paid no attention to the faults of their erring brethren. In 1784 it was resolved that members who were guilty of such excesses or vices as dancing, swearing, drinking, gambling, etc., were to be reproved publicly and were to make public confession that they had done wrong, that they were sorry for the same, that they asked pardon and would promise to avoid such sins in the future. In 1797 it was agreed that members who failed to pay their debts excluded themselves by their own conduct from the rights of membership. Hence they could be treated as non-members and might be sued at law. The church had its cases of discipline like other churches; the members erred in their ways as do those of other confessions. Many of these failings have been covered by the mantle of the past and the charitable hearts of the members blotted out the record of these shortcomings by a resolution adopted in 1805, that all reference in the minutes to former cases of discipline was to be stricken out and that in future such cases were not to be recorded. Work of a disciplinary character by deacons was thus consigned to oblivion and can not be referred to for precedence. Later on, however, the secretaries made such direct reference in their minutes to persons involved in discipline that it becomes easy to identify the parties under consideration. Cases of drunkenness, strife between members, improper use of money, unjust settlement of estates, fraud, etc., are noted in the minutes and in a few instances were continued from conference to conference. In these cases the action was calm, firm, charitable, deliberate. As a final resort after the failure of efforts at redemption, membership was cancelled. If those whose names were thus cancelled afterwards mended their ways, they were on proper expressions of penitence and confession received again. In the year 1846 the question was raised whether it would not be proper to substitute confession in conference for confession in open meeting before the society which had been the custom since 1784 but no change was effected. In 1852, however, a modification was brought about. It

was then unanimously resolved that, in cases of discipline
where the transgression does not bring a stain upon the
whole society, and the transgressor after due exhortation
professes proper penitence for his errors, no public confession should be required, but that if on account of the position assumed by the transgressor the matter had to be
brought before the conference, public confession should be
required.   This regulation was amended in 1865 so that
public announcement was to be made in case of private
confession.   The deacons were the ordinary channel
through which the church administered its cases of discipline.   At times committees were appointed to hear and
adjust cases or report the same to conference.

Church Business.—In the transaction of business as a
society, no distinction was or is made by Schwenkfelders, between minister and layman, all having equal rights
and privileges.   Regular general conferences have always
been held twice each year and special conferences as occasion required.   District conferences met from time to
time but seemingly no clear limitation of rights was made
between the general and district conference.   A moderator
and a secretary for each district were elected at the general
conference who usually, through reëlection, served many
years in succession.   The conferences were and are purely
democratic in theory, but in practice neither the young
male nor the female members seemingly took any great
part in the deliberations, during the early days of the
organization.   In the early minutes one reads that the
Haus-väter met and in the *Constitution and By-Laws*
of 1851 that the ministers are to be elected by the *Haus-
väter*.   This term should mean head of a house, but it
seems to have been used in the sense of male members.   It was made to mean members by the *Constitution*

and By-Laws of 1851 and male members by the English translation of the same in 1888. By the *Formula* of 1898 all members have equal rights and privileges. With respect to the transaction of business the following items may be noted. In 1782 it was agreed that it should be the duty of members to report to the secretary all subjects that they wished to have discussed at conference. Voting by ballot was agreed upon in 1783 with the proviso that the voting was to be secret and that those who were not in attendance at any particular conference might send their ballots. A resolution was adopted calling upon the moderator to make an address appropriate to the occasion, a summary of which was to be inserted in the minutes. In 1815 a question arose concerning the taking of testimony from parties who were not members of the society. It was agreed that such taking of testimony should be permissible but that such witnesses should not be admitted to the conference. At the conference in October, 1840, the custom of opening the session with prayer was made by resolution the established rule. At the fall conference, 1849, the question was raised whether the members were sufficiently acquainted with the constitution and regulations of the society and whether some persons might perhaps not have failed to become members through lack of such information. Accordingly, Reverend Joshua Schultz was authorized to prepare for publication a summary of the laws and regulations in force which was published under the title, *Constitution and By-Laws of the Schwenkfelder Society, 1851.*

Clothing. — The subject of clothing is a comparatively wide one and affords interesting material. The matter has been frequently discussed in public and in private, and has led to many a misunderstanding and censorious word. Individuals have run to extremes, but the conferences have as a rule been moderate in expression of opinion. In 1786 the following regulations were made with respect to clothing: (1) To discountenance all new modes, goods and styles that evidently only serve to clothe oneself in an extravagant and shameless manner to draw attention and to cultivate pride. (2) To permit members to use such styles in their clothing as are used generally by the good people of the community, forbidding unjust criticism of those who saw fit to adopt what all the common people of the vicinity were using. (3) To encourage the use of home-made clothing, of what members can raise and prepare for themselves. In 1842, after considerable discussion, the rules as given in the *Constitution and By-Laws of 1851*, were adopted as follows: "In order that with the mode of dress there may be no abuse practiced, it must be (1) comfortable, protecting both the body and the health, (2) it must be adapted to prevent evil desires, that those members are thereby covered whose sight might stir up impure desires. It may (3) be suitable to one's condition, that is, one may wear such clothing as other Christian and reasonable people of our condition, which best indicate and promote purity and humility. A Christian may (4) according to the circumstances of the times arrange his clothing, that he may for example go forth on a festival day different than upon a time of mourning. (5) He may also adapt himself to the custom of the time and place when such custom does not contain in itself anything that is sinful and does not conflict with propriety of conduct and decency, and whilst he does not place any holiness in this that he wears the old style of clothing, he nevertheless should guard against, at the same time, imitating all the new styles and much less will he make it his business to introduce new styles. They followed Pope's famous rule:

SPECIMEN OF SCHWENKFELDER PEN WORK, ORIGINAL IN FOUR COLORS.

"In words, as fashions, the same rule will hold ;
Alike fantastic, if too new of old ;
Be not the first by whom the new are tried,
Nor yet the last to lay the old aside."

It is probable that no attempt was at any time made to prescribe any religious garb or dress for the members, although custom had considerable influence over them even in this respect, and they seemingly were known by their clothing.

Memorial Day. — At the organization in 1782, the officiating at memorial days, observed since 1734, was by vote made a regular duty of the ministers, the distinctive religious tone of the services being thus preserved. Since 1791 the exercises with one exception have been held alternately in the meeting houses in the so-called Upper and Lower districts, on the twenty-fourth of September or on the twenty-fifth, if the twenty-fourth fell on Sunday. On account of having forenoon and afternoon sessions, provision for dinner at the house of worship has been made each year, presumably from the earliest observance of the day, so that worshippers would not be compelled to return to their homes for the noonday meal. After dismission the benches were covered with pure white linen, and on the table thus hurriedly prepared a simple repast of bread, butter and apple butter was soon spread and served, each helping himself with due decorum, and always heartily enjoyed. The exercises on these days have uniformly been of a devotional nature. The singing of hymns, the offering of prayers, the delivery of one or more sermons, the recounting of the cause of the observance of the day have always been a part of the program. In recent years there has been a tendency to widen the scope and influence of the day by trying to secure for it a more general attendance by descsendants irrepective of church connections.

The Sacraments. — A few words seem in place in this connection bearing on the use or non-use of the sacraments among the Schwenkfelders. In Europe they did not celebrate the sacraments because the church and the state would not allow them. Immediately after the migration they were in such a disorganized condition that the institution of such an important step could not be thought of. The lack of complete organization before 1782 was regarded a valid reason for not instituting the sacraments. This non-use had become a fixed and deeply-rooted habit at the time of the organization, the influence of which has scarcely disappeared at the present day. The position of the people on this subject at the time of the organization is indicated by the following facts. Christopher Schultz issued the first edition of his catechism in 1763. In revising it he had the advice of all the Schwenkfelders and the advantage of the use of it for twenty years. In the second edition, issued 1784, he answered affirmatively the following question, not found in the first edition : Does baptism, therefore, belong to the proper service of the gospel? In his *Compendium or Glaubenslehre,* Christopher Schultz, at the close of the discussion of the sacraments of the New Testament, says : "We should carefully guard ourselves against all abuse of this sacred institution in order that we may not fall under the condemnation of the Lord. Inattention to the same must be displeasing to the Lord and contrary to His will of love, since He well knew what is good and wholesome for us and serviceable to the increase of His Kingdom and Christian Communion." Directly after the organization in 1782, the ministers were instructed to preach several sermons each year on the sacraments. In response to this, Christopher Kriebel preached a series of twenty sermons, two each year, on Baptism and

the Lord's Supper.   George Kriebel preached a like series
and Christopher Schultz also began a series.   John Schultz
wrote a letter which was published in a German paper of
the year 1820, from which the following words are quoted :
" That the sacraments are not outwardly observed results
mainly from the cause that our forefathers in Germany did
not have the freedom to gather a church and observe them
as they deemed proper.   On their grievous journey from
Silesia to Saxony and thence across Holland and the sea
and during the first years in this country, the subject was
not to be thought of.   They thus had to work their way
through for more than 200 years without such holy services.   At their closer organization in 1782, omission had
become custom that has continued since, but we flatter ourselves with the hope that such things may in the future not
be left out of consideration."   About the year 1840, a considerable discussion arose about the institution of the sacraments which finally led to the resolution that the ministers should have the right to baptize and hold communion
with all the believers (members) who sincerely desired the
same.   During the years 1856–58, another period of discussion manifested itself, the outcome of which was that
the ministers were appointed a committee to draw up rules
and regulations for the proper observance of the sacraments.   The committee met, and after some effort, com-
promised on a report, and then the matter came to a rest
again.   Agitation started up anew about the year 1874,
which led to the publishing of the committee report of
1858 and of two sermons by Weiss and Hoffman and
finally resulted in the institution of the sacraments in the
Lower District at the private house of Anthony K. Heebner
in 1877.   A wave of earnest discussion, argument and re-
crimination followed which occasioned the appointment of

a compromise committee in 1888. This committee went to work, toiled on and finally made its report, which was adopted and printed in 1894. By virtue of the committee report, opportunity was given in the Upper District for baptism and communion and has been regularly continued since. The charge has often been made that the Schwenkfelders are opposed to the sacraments, but the charge can not be substantiated. The published writings, the many unpublished manuscripts, the action of conferences, verified traditions, are all evidence to the contrary. Many a vigorous protest may be found against the abuse of the sacraments in these references, but against the proper use thereof none whatever. The fact is not overlooked that all along individuals have maintained the views of the Friends about the use of externals, but these never represented the consensus of opinion of their fellow-members as a body.

It will not be amiss to close this chapter by quoting the following from a recent tract:

"Present Modes of Activity.

" 1. The ministry — jealously guarded as to purity of doctrine of incumbents by the members of the churches.

" 2. Public worship — evangelical, simple, flexible as to time and manner.

" 3. Sunday-schools — maintained since the migration in 1734.

" 4. Catechetical instruction — adapted to train the young in the doctrines of the church.

" 5. Charity Fund — founded in 1774, through which the church has always cared for its unfortunate members.

" 6. Perkiomen Seminary — a preparatory school for both sexes.

" 7. Board of Missions — incorporated in 1895.

" 8. Board of Publication — the publishing medium, conducting the work on the *Corpus Schwenkfeldianorum.*

" 9. Ladies' Aid Societies — organized to direct and undertake certain lines of charitable work.

" 10. Christian Endeavor Societies — working in harmony with the United Society."

CHAPTER VIII.

The Relation Between the Schwenkfelders and Zinzendorf in Pennsylvania.

Y object in this chapter will be to summarize the chief items of interest relating to the connection between Count Zinzendorf as their former friend in need and the Schwenkfelders after their migration in 1734. The earlier experiences have been touched upon in a different connection. For a discussion of the general development of Moravian church life in America, the kind reader is referred to special books on the subject.

In *Memorials of the Moravian Church*, Vol. I., page 157, the statement is made that "George Bönisch, Christopher Baus and Christopher Wiegner arrived at Philadelphia on the *St. Andrew*, Captain Stedman, September 22, 1734. This vessel brought the Schwenkfelders whom Zinzendorf had received at Berthelsdorf, on their banishment from Silesia. Bönisch accompanied them to Pennsylvania at their request and during their stay resided at Wiegner's." These are the three to whom Cranz refers in his history in these words: " Three brothers were sent with them (the Schwenkfelders) who at the request of them were to aid in caring for the temporal and spiritual welfare of the Schwenkfelders." Recognition of such a mission and request in the writings of the Schwenkfelders has not been brought to light. Augustus Gottlieb Spangenberg, A.M., of the University of Jena, later Bishop of the Moravian Church, than whom Count Zinzendorf alone stood higher in the councils of the Moravian Church, had expected to accompany the Schwenkfelders because he had noticed in them an earnest Christian spirit, but when knowledge came that they were to go to Pennsylvania and not to Georgia as he himself had hoped, Spangenberg was delegated to conduct a company of Moravian emigrants to Georgia. While Schwenkfelders were founding new homes in Pennsylvania, Spangenberg was caring for the band of Moravian immigrants who had arrived in Savannah, March, 1735. After he had established the infant colony and had been ordained a presbyter of the Moravian Church by Bishop Nitschman who had recently arrived in the colony of Georgia, he left March 15, 1736, with letters of recommendation from Governor Oglethorpe to Thomas Penn to take up his mission proper in Pennsylvania. Christopher Wiegner must have been expecting him on his farm at Towamencin about this time. He wrote in his diary, April 3 : " I came home tired from plowing but said that if Spangenberg were in the city, I would go that night to see him." The next day Wiegner said he must come. Hardly had he said this when in stepped Spangenberg and surprised them as the family

INTERIOR OF SALFORD MEETINGHOUSE.

SCHWENKFELDER GRAVEYARD AT CHESTNUT HILL.

sat at the dinner table. From this time on until his recall to Europe in 1739 he made his home with Wiegner, going away of course for longer and shorter periods on account of his duties as demands came upon him.

The object of the coming of Spangenberg, as of Wiegner, Baus and Bönisch, was in part at least to bring the Schwenkfelders over to the Moravian faith. On the day following his arrival he wrote: "I will visit the people, offer them my peace, place myself at their service, hear, ask and answer as it may please them, wishing that God Himself may open a door." During his stay he would, as opportunity presented itself, take part in the operations of the farm. Reichel says: "He took many practical lessons in ploughing, threshing and other agricultural elements, by which he became well qualified for future usefulness in the economies of Bethlehem and Nazareth." To his dying day he looked back with pleasure to the happy and peaceful days spent on the Wiegner farm. Wiegner makes many references to these experiences to which space permits but fragmentary reference.

On the fifth of May, 1736, Bishop David Nitschman arrived and on the eighth went to "Cainstook" accompanied by Spangenberg. The Bishop left again on the twenty-second of May. About the middle of the month Spangenberg wrote that the Schwenkfelders who lived greatly scattered received him in love on his visits and that he hoped that many might be converted. Wiegner relates that they were at Kriebel's (probably Melchior Kriebel's) on the twentieth of June, 1736, and that Spangenberg spoke and Bönisch prayed. George Weiss soon called at their home and remonstrated with them saying that "we disturbed them and that we should let them alone, that they would leave us alone, that we were not agreed and that he knew of many people who prayed and acted very earnestly of whom terrible things were heard later; and that it was in vain to unite the Schwenkfelders and the Moravians. * * * Because Spangenberg spoke very mildly and peaceably we would have to wait a few years to see whether he would continue thus." On the ninth of July, Weiss made a call at Wiegner's and had an extended discussion of doctrinal points with Spangenberg and they seem to have been quite friendly. The next day Spangenberg left for St. Thomas deputized by Nitschman to hold a visitation. Thus he was called away from his work for a season. He returned in November, following.

In February, 1737, George Neisser arrived at Wiegner's. He had been deputized by the brethren in Georgia to report their distress to Spangenberg and to urge him to repair to London to lay their grievances before the "Trustees for the Colony of Georgia." Wiegner relates that he and Spangenberg early in March discussed the advisability of visiting Georgia, that in April after consultation, the Schwenkfelders advised his going, upon which he made up his mind to go. On the twenty-ninth of April, Weiss and Spangenberg started afoot for Germantown, arriving there about midnight. Wiegner records thanks for the blessed communion on the way. In May, Spangenberg sailed for Georgia accompanied by John Eckstein. In August, Wiegner wrote a letter to Count Zinzendorf in which he related Spangenberg's affairs and requested instruction concerning certain letters and the standing of George Bönisch, since it was good neither for him nor for the others that he did not know how long he was to stay. He also spoke of the kind reception given to Spangenberg by the Schwenkfelders.

Spangenberg returned from Georgia to Wiegner's early in September, 1737. In December the two went to Philadelphia. They seem to have had a warm discussion, Spangenberg wanting to start special regulations in external matters, like eating, sleeping and clothing. Wiegner wrote: " God gave grace that we could understand each other, and Spangenberg made promises and we loved each other and rejoiced together." On the thirtieth of December Wiegner entered this interesting note in his diary: " Started on our journey. Neither of us felt well, yet we had a prompting towards such a journey. The Lord made all things work together for the best. Until we came to the Swamp, we were in great distress spiritually. We sang and prayed in our misery and comforted eath other and the grace of love and communion manifested itself strongly on the whole journey." On the seventh of January they came back from the visit in blessing and peace. It is probably with reference to this trip that George Neisser says: " Spangenberg and Christopher Wiegner at one time made a visitation to Falckner Swamp, Oley and Conestoga among the Ephrata brethren and among the so-called ' New-mooners ' in Conestoga Swamp with John Zimmerman and found many upright souls, but greatly divided with respect to theories and non-essentials."

Wiegner made the following entry in his diary January 19, 1738 : " Attended services at M. Kriebel's. George Weiss said the Bible was a sealed book and was only for the saints (*Heilig-recommandirte*) — hence his 1,500 hymns and other literature. This affected me so much that I made a loud exclamation and Br. Sp. (Brother Spangenberg) did the same which stirred up considerable uproar. George Weiss wrote a letter to which we replied again." This stormy meeting meant much. An extensive correspondence followed. It was more than a mere clashing between Weiss and Spangenberg. It was rather a clashing between two great systems of thought — Weiss defending Casper Schwenkfeld and Spangenberg representing Zinzendorf, a professed adherent of the Lutheran faith, although the great defender of the Moravians. The following April Wiegner wrote: "George Weiss rejects us," and Spangenberg wrote: "The Schwenkfelders form themselves wholly into a sect and completely close themselves against all others who do not approve of their cause, whereby consciences are bound and the spirit of Christ is quenched. I can reject no brother nor separate myself from him to win others and be a means of salvation to them. The Lord will show what the outcome will be. We do not say much, but have expressed ourselves both orally and in writing." Reichel says: "In 1738, when visiting the Schwenkfelders for the third time, he (*Spangenberg*) complained of their exclusive sectarian spirit, by which the consciences are burdened; but it is still more likely that Spangenberg, 'still too learned to be an apostle' (as Zinzendorf expressed it) and lacking experience, did not always meet them, and especially their minister, George Weiss, with that Christian candor and liberality which alone awakens confidence, and which in later years was the brightest ornament of Bro. Spangenberg's career." In Fresenius we find these words: "At first for a considerable time Spangenberg attended their meetings, adopted their mode of dress, associated much with them, and they permitted this for a time, although they knew his principles while yet in the old country, but they were disinclined to enter into a more intimate familiarity with and submission to him, until at last George Weiss, their preacher, who was not at all inclined to adopt the Herrnhuter form, and espe cially not their outward ceremonies and manner of teaching, forbade his further teaching or acting in their meetings."

George Neisser, who lived with Wiegner for a while, says: " Through condescendence towards the Schwenkfelders the whole company (Wiegner, Spangenberg and the others at Wiegner's house) attended their services and in clothing and other matters adapted themselves to them. But when it was perceived that this condescension and other inducements to love as well as the efforts to win them would bear no fruit, a gradual withdrawal took place." Sunday services were then instituted at Wiegner's, to which particularly on festival occasions and in summer time there came among others : From Skippack : Heinrich Frey, Johannes Kooken, George Merkel, Christian Weber, Jost Schmidt, Willhelm Bossens, Jost Becker; from Friedrichstown (Frederick Township): Heinrich Antes, Wilhelm Frey, George Stiefel, Heinrich Holstein, Andreas Frey; from Matetsche (Methacton): Matthias Gmelen, Abraham Wagner; from Oley: John Bertolet, Franz Ritter and Wilhelm Pott; from Germantown: Johannes Bechtel, Johann Adam Gruber, Blasius Mackinet and George Benzel. Monthly conferences were also held, which continued until 1740. It was probably in this connection that the name " The Associated Brethren of the Skippack" arose.

On the fifteenth of March, 1739, Wiegner wrote that Spangenberg had received a call to Germany and that they were thus placed in great straits (*Wir stehen sehr in der enge*). The following August, Spangenberg according to Reichel left for Europe without having had the pleasure of seeing much fruit for his labors. It used to be said that he came to Pennsylvania a very wise man, but had returned a much wiser man. Before his return he wrote : " My plan is to declare freely to all that in Christ Jesus naught but a new creature avails, such a one we will consider a brother ; others are but men of the world and cannot stand before God. We will not concern ourselves whether a man has a particular name but whether he believes on the Lord Jesus Christ and walks in the law of love." These words can easily be duplicated from the writings of Casper Schwenkfeld. The words do honor to any follower of the Lord. One might almost be tempted to ask, Did a Schwenkfelder utter these words? In fact we find that Zinzendorf told Eckstein that Spangenberg was a Schwenkfelder. What he meant by such a statement is not made clear. Isaac Schultz wrote in 1839 that Spangenberg loved and read Schwenkfeld's writings, and that he would have remained with his friends if he had not been called away. Verification of this statement has not been possible from other sources. What would have been the result if he had not been called away? What would have been the outcome if George Weiss had been a mercenary, and sought to draw the Associated Brethren of the Skippack into the Schwenkfelder fold?

April 25, 1740, the remnant of the Moravian colony in Georgia came to Philadelphia on board of the sloop *Savanna* with Whitefield, the well-known leader of the Methodists. Reichel says : " They were greatly disappointed at not finding either Spangenberg, who had left for Europe or Bishop Nitschman, whose early arrival was expected. They went to Wiegner's, next to Henry Antes and then back again to Germantown." Meanwhile Mr. Whitefield had bought 5,000 acres of land in Northampton County for the purpose of erecting a school for negroes. On May 5, he came to Wiegner's plantation in Skippack to see Peter Böhler concerning the intended building. Many people assembled to see and hear the famous Mr. Whitefield, who preached to them in English followed by Peter Böhler in a German address. In Whitefield's journal are found these words : " Preached at Skippack sixteen miles from Montgomery where the Dutch people live. It was seemingly a very wilderness part of the country ; but there were not less I believe than 2,000 hearers." Wiegner's diary closes with April, 1739, so that it furnishes no information concerning this or subsequent visits or affairs. From other sources we learn, however, that Eschenbach, Rauch, Anne Nitschmann, Molter, Zeisberger and other Moravians enjoyed the hospitality of the home of Christopher Wiegner, his sister and mother.

Zinzendorf's missionary zeal is appropriately expressed in his own words of August, 1741 : " I am destined by the Lord to proclaim the message of the death and blood of Jesus." He longed to preach Christ crucified and to build up a true church unto the Lord. Reichel says : " Zinzendorf was of the opinion that the best field for unrestrained general activity for the Kingdom of God would be in Pennsylvania ; for in a country and among a people where there were as yet no ecclesiastical organizations whatever there could not be hindrances such as he met elsewhere — hindrances founded upon and emanating from ecclesiastical usages and customs of old standing. Therefore if anywhere on earth his ideal of ' a church of God in the Spirit' could be realized, Pennsylvania, he thought, might be that country." With this in mind he came to Pennsylvania in December, 1741, to labor among the diverse churches and sects scattered throughout Pennsylvania. Within ten days after his arrival he called on Wiegner and preached a sermon on John III. 16 and

Matt. XVI. 19 which seems to have given scant satisfaction. Wiegner's "Associated Brethren of the Skippack" probably formed a factor in the count's decision to come to Pennsylvania. Hence it was but the natural thing to make such a prompt call at Wiegner's home. A few days later, December 15, O. S., a call was issued signed by Henry Antes one of the frequenters at the meetings at Wiegner's for a general meeting at Germantown of members of all denominations "not for the purpose of disputing but in order to treat peaceably concerning the most important articles of faith and to ascertain how far they might all agree in the most essential points for the purpose of promoting mutual love and forbearance."

In pursuance of the call a synod was therefore held in Germantown on New Year's day, O. S. Christopher Wiegner, according to some reports, seems to have been one of the important members of the gathering. Christopher Saur said concerning this synod: "The Schwenkfelders knew him (Zinzendorf) and had lived with him. Of these none came. Two who lived in Germantown were prevailed upon to attend, but when they saw that they were only wanted in order that it might be heralded abroad that they too had attended they went home." It seems that Saur did not class Wiegner as a Schwenkfelder or did not know of his attendance. The scant attention given the gathering by the Schwenkfelders, the displeasure aroused by their not migrating to Georgia originally, the non-responsiveness to the labors of Bönisch and Spangenberg, the sly sycophancy of others, probably put Zinzendorf into a frame of mind that on slight provocation might lead him to imprudent acts and this indeed happened all too soon.

On Epiphany, January 6, Zinzendorf preached the second time at Wiegner's and was listened to by the

Schwenkfelders who rejoiced to see their former guardian angel and benefactor. It seems that on the same day eight of them called upon him at his house in Germantown. Both here and at Wiegner's controversy arose. What took place was written out by the Schwenkfelders and later published. Zinzendorf questioned them concerning their confession of faith, their organization, their hymns and other points. He said Schwenkfeld taught error, rejected word and outward things or services, that George Weiss led the people around by the nose and taught errors, that it was easier to preach to Satan than to them, that he had power over them and was bound to save their souls, that he would not rest until he had destroyed them and torn their children from them, that he would use all his powers to tear souls from them and to save the children from hell. They politely answered his questions, saying among other things: "After many attacks upon us and our truth we left Germany and should it be that here also we could not remain in peace, there would no doubt be found again some other little spot for us. We do not intend to depart from our confession." To say the least, Zinzendorf did not show the wisdom of a serpent nor the harmlessness of a dove in thus attacking a body of people so well spoken of as the Schwenkfelders. A few days later he and Bishop Nitschman called upon John Eckstein, who had accompanied Spangenberg to Georgia. Here the Schwenkfelders were again discussed, Zinzendorf reiterating what he had said before to the Schwenkfelders while Eckstein defended them, upon which the count became quite wrathful, saying that he had power over them and that he would pray the Lord to cast them out of his mouth.

Some time after this Zinzendorf actually consulted a magistrate concerning his imagined power over them and

8

was told that if he had paid no ship-passage for them, he
could have no power over them. What the outcome
would have been had the passage been paid by the count,
no one can tell. Would they have been sold as redemptioners? Would they have gone to Georgia instead of
Pennsylvania, there to perish as did some of the Moravians?
Zinzendorf's course of conduct was adapted to cause perplexity leading to conference and consultation. He was
continually making threats, seeking, as it appeared to the
Schwenkfelders, to tempt them to commit some outward act
against him but they, as was their custom, were seeking as
much as lay in their power to live at peace with all men
and particularly with him.

The second synod met January 14 and 15 at the house
of George Hübner in Falckner Swamp. George was a
son of Doctor Melchior Hübner who had migrated with
the Schwenkfelders but who was not in harmony with the
leaders and was not considered as one of the Schwenkfelders at the time of his death in 1738. The son was undoubtedly influenced by the father and thus was probably
not a strict Schwenkfelder. He as a miller was a business
partner of Henry Antes and also a considerable land-
holder. Wiegner attended the synod and was granted the
freedom of the synods, being one of the members at liberty
to attend without further notice. The Schwenkfelders
did not send delegates to this nor to any subsequent synod.
The tumult incited by Zinzendorf on Epiphany must have
been noised about and must have aroused attention even
among the members of the synod and was in itself ample
excuse for non-attendance.

At the third conference held in Oley, February 10–12,
the proposition was made that if the Schwenkfelders had
any complaints against Brother Ludwig (Zinzendorf) they
should present themselves at the next synod.

The fourth synod met in Germantown, March 10–12. A letter written by Casper Kriebel dated, " Domentz, March 7, 1742," replying to one by Christopher Schultz, raising the question of making a defense against Zinzendorf, contained the words : " It is the opinion of myself and some others that it is not advisable to attend said conference. Hitherto we have had nothing to do with him. He indeed makes pretensions against us, but these are European and not American." According to Reichel, " when Zinzendorf entered and found that only those had made their appearance who were really one in spirit — the Mennonites and Schwenkfelders having sent no deputies — he felt that the proper objects of these meetings would not be gained and proposed to dissolve the meeting at once, but this proposition was overruled by the synod."

The day previous to the opening of the synod, Wiegner and Zinzendorf discussed the Schwenkfelders and Wiegner told the count that in certain respects he had labored under misapprehensions. The result was a letter by Zinzendorf dated " Germantown, March 20, 1742," (N. S.) He recounted the experiences at the previous Epiphany, tried to justify his own conduct, saying among other things : " I declared to your attending deputies * * * how I thought to proceed. * * * I would fix a time of three months for your false teachers, unconverted overseers and blind leaders ; if during that time some one who knows the cross of Jesus would take you in charge, convert some of you, introduce the holy sacraments and thus make you capable of the name of a church, then I would have to let you stand in the Lord, for you would then be an ordinary religion. But in case the heretofore and still existing confusion should continue and according to your own confession to me no one became converted, false doctrine should continue in vogue, the sacraments remain absolutely abolished and when one inquires of you for foundations, nothing be left but the bare name of the sect, the particular dress and perhaps an empty word sound about the dead letter, inner word, spirit and the like; then rather than permit you to become scattered here and there to desert and connect with other sects to become false separatists and thus to permit your entire ruin, I would concern myself earnestly about you with this purpose to make a beginning while you were here, to visit you specifically, to gather and improve you, to remove the hirelings from you in case they withstood me, to tear the sheep out of their mouths. * * * I therefore wanted to remind you that the time is approaching and terminates on the sixth of April, when you are again invited to a conference." [1]

To this letter Balzer Hoffman and other sundry friends politely replied that they would not attend the conference or synod, that they commended themselves to God and that they conceded to all the privilege of acting as seemed best to them. Zinzendorf replied again as follows: "While I hereby charge you publicly before the all-seeing eyes of God the Saviour as well as before every honorable man that you have committed the spiritual and temporal care of your people to me in writing in case you should dwell outside of my territory and particularly outside of Europe and indeed partly in naming Pennsylvania. But I do not wish to lay the writing before you, because you treat me with sophistical artifices and I (the appointee of Jesus as Reformer of the Schwenkfelder religion) being obliged to proceed apostolically desire that you give me the following

---

[1] "It was an empty threat that these people should fear and at once prostrate themselves, for they did not come and paid no attention to his dictatorial counsels, but remained quietly away from him and since that time he could not undertake anything further against them."

written obligation under your name that until after your death you will take the charge upon yourselves; in that event this paper will serve you as a strong obligation on my part that I will defer my services as reformer of the Schwenkfelder religion until your death, unless it should happen that some souls among you would request me to perform such service whom I would at all times accept as my children," etc.

The following is the form of release proposed: "We, the undersigned, release Count Louis von Zinzendorf in the sincerest and most effective manner before God and man of and from all temporal and spiritual care of the Schwenkfelders in America during the term of our lives." The following rejoinder was then given by the Schwenkfelders: "Out of veneration for your person we have in sincerity replied to all demands heretofore made upon us but finding that our simple yet truthful declarations are construed as sophistry, we are compelled hereafter absolutely to decline to take notice of any and every importunity that may be made, both written and oral, until we are shown that written power of our submission which we are said to have executed. It is not the accusation but the evidence that proves the case. We do not believe in that entrusted instruction from Christ against our religion. We decline the demand, we have neither the bestowed nor assumed power or arbitrariness to treat with our people in the manner indicated; it would appear neither formal nor proper, but rather it would appear foolish. By the help of God we shall remain with ours, thank Him for our liberty, place our trust in His provident care and commit ourselves with all that may impend to Him. For what length of time that entrusted reformation is to be suspended does not give us any concern. With this simple declaration we merely make known that we can not assume, much less assent to what we are charged with. We can not imagine why such a binding obligation has not been shown ere this: as we frankly made known our intentions and commenced our journey publicly."

At the seventh synod the views of the members were expressed concerning the religious state of nine denominations in Pennsylvania. Of the Schwenkfelders the conclusion was in part as follows: "The Schwenkfelders so-called are in a lamentable condition. They have no system of their own. In Germany they allow their children to be baptized; here they do not. Those who offered to aid them they have rejected. Brother Thurnstein (Zinzendorf) brought with him and beside received here such views of them as misled him into a severity which they indeed deserved, but which their accusers deserved much more. * * * He also sought a release from them showing that they would decline his duty towards them during their lives; this they returned unsigned. He has at this time a definite assurance from a sufficient number of them that they neither need him nor expect to unite with him."

The seventh was the last of the synods in which Zinzendorf participated and also marks the time when first the Schwenkfelders could feel themselves entirely free from the power of Zinzendorf. For sixteen years had they in an unorganized condition withstood his efforts at " conversion " and successfully stood by the faith of the fathers placed in their hands as a sacred trust according to their view. A heart of charity will not impugn the motives or his love, but perchance may see in him one of God's lambs wrapped in wolf's clothing, and actuated by a feudalistic spirit entirely foreign to the genius of the church and state in Pennsylvania.

To a Schwenkfelder who fully appreciated his own system of doctrine, it would have seemed preposterous to adopt as his spiritual guide and teacher, Zinzendorf who, as report has it, taught that there were but two churches, the Roman Catholic and the Moravian, the former even having lost its power, that the children of Moravian parents did not need regeneration, that baptism of water was regeneration, that claimed to be the " appointee of Jesus as Reformer of the Schwenkfelder religion."

To guard against unwarranted inferences it will be in place to say in conclusion that the most cordial relation has always existed between Schwenkfelders and Moravians and that it is to be hoped that the same may continue in years to come.

WHEEL FOR SPINNING OR TWISTING WOOL.

CHAPTER IX.

NOWLEDGE is power and its acquisition a Christian duty. In studying the history of secular education among the Schwenkfelders as a body, one finds comparatively little material relating to the first thirty years after the immigration. It is evident that the immigrant Schwenkfelders were not of a low type of intelligence. Very few of them made their " mark " at the time of their taking the pledge of allegiance. Their religious leaders, Weiss, Hoffman and Schultz, probably aided the respective communities in winning the elements of a practical education in the common branches. Christopher Schultz in his *Historische Anmerkungen* says that about the year 1764 there was considerable deliberation with respect to the establishment of a school system for and by the Schwenkfelders. The necessity for such schools was laid before the heads of families in a series of questions. A meeting was thereupon held on the first of March, 1764, and money pledged for the support of the schools. In June another meeting was held when articles of agreement were adopted and the system was inaugurated.

In the deliberations of June, the following principles were agreed to, written out quite fully and illustrated by references to a number of authorities :

1. Man by nature is lost, but is intended by God to be eternally happy.

2. It is the duty of parents to bring up their children in the fear of God and in useful knowledge.

3. A system of public schools is necessary to lighten, but it can not remove, the duty of parents in this respect.

4. It is the object of schools to lead children into the wisdom of God and the possession of useful knowledge.

5. Specifically it is their object to educate in godliness, learning and virtue.

6. This principle concerning the object of schools is founded on God.

7. The essential conditions of good schools are competent teachers, order and regulations, a true fear of God, impartation of useful knowledge, care of teachers.

8. A teacher ought to be godly, educated and of good repute.

9. A faithful teacher must seek the true welfare of his pupils.

10. It is necessary for parents and teachers to agree as to methods to bring about the best results.

11. The moral training of children must not be overlooked.

12. The reading of God's Word and the study of the catechism should not be omitted from schools.

13. Reading and writing the English and German languages, arithmetic and geography and other useful branches should be studied.

TITLE PAGE "GOSHENHOPPEN SCHUL BUCH" OR MINUTE BOOK OF
SCHOOL-SYSTEM.

14. Provision should be made for the support of the teacher.

At the time of the adoption of the afore-mentioned principles, the following regulations were also adopted :

Certain Agreements and Fundamental Articles for the establishment, support and continuation of a school-system in the districts of Skippack and Goshenhoppen as they were agreed upon and determined by and between the contributors thereto this thirteenth day of June, 1764.

WHEREAS, the faithful training of the young in reading, writing and the study of the languages and useful sciences, according to sex, age and standing and their instruction in the principles of morality, virtue and true religion contribute very much to the prosperity and welfare of every community, which can be accomplished in no way better than by the establishment of schools under wise and proper regulations adapted to such undertaking and,

WHEREAS, the small community of people, known by the name " Schwenkfelders " has hitherto been under great inconvenience for the education of their children in the useful elements referred to above through want of well-regulated schools ;

Therefore, they took the matter to heart and met on the first day of March, 1764, in Skippack and earnestly deliberated how and in what form schools might be established among them whereupon they concluded that it would be most convenient to collect and establish a fund from the proceeds of which the most, even if not all the expenses for the support of such schools could be met, annually their deliberations agreeing on the following conditions and terms. The above-named took into consideration their insignificant numbers and means in comparison with the heavy expenses that would be incurred by such schools and concluded that in view of these circumstances, it would be advantageous to the encouragement of subscriptions and the collection of a larger amount to regard the sums brought together thus as a loan conditioned as follows: The said contributors and subscribers give their respective contributions to the fund as a loan for a period of sixteen years reckoned from the sixteenth day of May, 1764. Such sum shall be under the management of certain trustees in order that the interest thereof at 5 per cent. per annum may be applied to the support of the said schools in the hope and trust in divine direction that meanwhile such necessary and important undertaking may gradually be further encouraged by those favorably inclined and supported in true Christian spirit by gifts and loans so that it may be continually strengthened. It is their purpose not only to support the said fund according to their ability but also to commend the same to their friends as best they may from time to time. For it is their aim, agreement and intention that as long as there are children to be educated and as long as the fund can be administered under the manifest favor of God, the said fund shall be continued and the whole undertaking shall be conducted by God's blessing unalterably according to the following regulations.

Wherefore let all whom it may concern know that we the above-mentioned contributors earnestly desire that this undertaking may not be hindered or rendered ineffectual and that it may be conducted according to principles of prudence and discretion. Hence we have agreed upon the following fundamental articles, regulations and rules to provide a prudent management of the fund and good government of the schools before mentioned. Our true idea and plainly evident wish is not to be changed or perverted respecting this but is to continue the same and remain in full power forever.

1. Since the originators and contributors to the said fund are of the people called Schwenkfelders, they regard the undertaking as theirs and desire that the trustees elected for the control of the fund and supervision of the schools may at all times be prudent and reputable men of the said community. But the idea and intention is that the said school system shall be open to the children of the parents of any denomination, whoever they may be, under this condition that they pay for the instruction of their children, and that they and their children shall regulate and conduct themselves according to the necessary regulations hereby presented, as well as those that may be made hereafter by the trustees hereinafter mentioned. Whereby, however, the impartial instruction according to the religion of each as much as relates to the schools shall not be hindered.

2. On the second Monday in the month of March of each year forever between the hours of 10 and 2 of the said day the contributors to such school system (but they must be such of whatever religious society as have already subscribed or hereafter contribute, either to lend for a time £20 or more or to donate £2 in Pennsylvania currency or more to be expended for said school system) shall have the right to assemble at one of the school houses designated by the trustees, and then and there they or the majority of those that have met shall vote by ballot for trustees of the said school system for the succeeding year. The number of trustees shall be five, or as many as the contributors may agree upon, and these shall be reputable persons of the community.

3. The said trustees or the majority of them shall have power and authority to make, order and establish good and

necessary rules and regulations for the good government of said schools, the officers of the schools and the scholars who shall be amenable to the trustees collectively and individually, yet with the condition that such rules and regulations be in harmony with sound reason and the general regulations of this general plan.

4. The said trustees or the majority of them shall have full power and authority to examine and adjust all important differences that may arise between the teachers and pupils, or their masters, parents or those who may be in authority over them, and the complaints of such as may feel wronged, either teachers or pupils, or any of them; yet with this condition that by this article or whatever is included in it, it is not intended that those in authority — the teachers — shall be restrained from administering such reasonable and moderate chastisement as they may deem necessary.

5. The said trustees or the majority of them shall from time to time elect and make agreement with school teachers and for just cause dismiss and discharge the same; also dismiss and discharge unruly scholars and such as will not conduct themselves in accord with the afore-mentioned rules and regulations, as well as those who in unjust matters are not properly admonished by parent, guardian, master or mistress. In their election of school officers or schoolmasters due care must be taken that persons of education, wisdom, and unaffected piety and virtue are preferred and that such are avoided as are known to be selfish, quarrelsome and without affection. As far as possible they shall adapt themselves to the instructions of the contributors as agreed upon in June, 1764.

6. The said trustees or the majority of them shall have full power and authority to have in their care, protection

and management the aforesaid fund and all money belonging to the same. They shall keep an accurate account of the same and of their financial transactions, giving income and expenses, loans and all the circumstances relating to the same. The obligation and security which they give as trustees shall be ample and binding both as to themselves and their successors in office.

7. The said trustees or the majority of them shall faithfully use or invest all such money or income of such money as many be contributed to said school system by will, present or loan at all times as they may deem best for the true welfare of the same in accordance with the herein-mentioned regulations, unless those that bequeath, present or loan the money give order how the money shall be used, which orders shall always be minutely followed in so far as they are not contrary to the herein-embraced regulations.

8. The said schools shall be visited once in each month by at least two of said trustees in order that both teacher and pupil may do their duty. The trustees or the majority of them shall meet whenever the said visiting trustees find occasion to call them together and then to order and regulate the affairs for which they are appointed and for which the said visiting trustees may have called them. They shall keep a book at the expense of the community in which to note and record all such matters as they may have agreed upon with respect to the schools at their meetings as well as accounts of all money which they receive, expend or pay out from time to time. The said book shall be laid before the annual meeting of the contributors for inspection.

9. In case, however, it should be discovered, seen and recognized by the contributors, contrary to all expectation, that the work thus instituted, the said school system, is

more harmful than beneficial to the worthy cause hereby indicated, it is herewith agreed and resolved that in such event the whole matter shall be brought to an end and restitution shall be made to each contributor or his heirs of the money donated and of the obligations and securities except what may have been expended.

10. It is further the sense and idea that the contributors or a majority of them assembled at any general meeting shall have the right to make such further regulations and to do and provide all such things as from time to time may be found serviceable to the well-being and convenience of the said undertaking — the school-system.

In witness hereof there follow herewith the names of the founders, subscribers and supporters of the said school-system together with the amount of money subscribed by each.

Christoph Schultz	£50 a loan		Casper Kribel	£50 a loan	
George Schultz	30	"	George Kribel Jun.	30	"
George Schultz, Jun.	50	"	Abraham Kribel	30	"
Melchior Schultz	50	"	George Anders Sen.	5	"
Barbara Yeakel	40	"	George Anders Jun.	20	"
Andreas Warmer	20	"	Melcher Krebel	20	"
David Schultz	10	"	Casper Seibt	30	"
Christoph Krause	40	"	Christoph Neumann	20	"
Christoph Yeakel	50	"	David Neuman	25	"
Balthasar Yeakel	10	"	Heinrich Schneider	20	"
Johannes Yeakel	50	"	Abraham Yeakel	20	"
George Heydrich	6 a donation		Gregorius Schultz	20	"
George Kriebel	30 a loan		Rosina Wiegner	30 Nov. 27,	
Christoph Kribel	30	"		1766	
Christoph Hoffman	20	"	Andreas Haag	4 a donation	
Hansz Chr. Huebner	30	"	Summa	£840.0.0.	

The showing made by the subscription list is quite creditable, although about twenty-five families were not represented. Of these, some had moved away, some had no means, a few may not have been entirely in sympathy with the movement and some did not join in any work of the Schwenkfelders, not being looked upon as being of the Schwenkfelders. The 840 pounds originally subscribed was reduced to less than 800 by the withdrawal of a few subscriptions.

In this effort they had the example of practically all the churches around them : Mennonite, Reformed, Lutheran, Quaker, Moravian, Presbyterian, Episcopalian, Catholic — schools being conducted by all of these denominations. It is not unlikely that they received suggestions and inspiration from the establishment of the Germantown Academy, 1761. Unlike these churches, however, they could not look to the fatherland for aid, for there they had none to aid them. They could not look to the provincial government for it aided none educationally. They had the example of the religious and secular community to use the lottery for raising money, for they had seen churches, parsonages, schoolhouses, paved streets and general public improvements made by raising money through such means. They chose the cheapest and best way of giving — by giving. Space forbids any detailed references to the prominent and commendable features of the plan which will become evident to the attentive reader on its perusal.

The first election of officers took place August 10, 1764, when the following trustees were chosen : Melchior Schultz, Christopher Schultz, Christopher Yeakel, George Kriebel and Casper Kriebel. The first teachers were John Davis and John Doerbaum. The former conducted a school for six months in the home of Christopher Schultz at a salary of £20 ($53.33) and board for the term ; the latter, for the same time in the house of George Anders for £10 ($26.66) and board, light and fuel. Melchior Wiegner and Melchior Schultz jointly conveyed to the

9

trustees, September 24, 1764, two acres and fifty perches of meadow land for the benefit and use of the schools and the school teacher. The trustees made improvements on the land the following spring. The land reverted to the original owners seemingly by provision of the deed of conveyance.

The first school-house was built in 1765, in Towamencin, close to where the Schwenkfelder meeting house now stands, and a dwelling house for the teacher was erected a little later. Verbal promises were made at the time which, when it was proposed to put them into writing, led to misunderstandings followed by recriminations affecting even the attendance at the meetings for worship on Sunday. The following spring (1766), at a business meeting, several of the subscribers said they were a thousand times sorry that they had joined in the movement to establish the schools. The dissatisfaction had not even died out in 1771 when a censorious paper was sent to the trustees of the Goshenhoppen district.

One of the early teachers gave considerable trouble to the trustees on account of his doctrinal standpoint. He was a great friend of the writings of Dippel and Edelman, and went so far as to quote objectionable passages from their writings in setting the copy-books of the pupils. It is needless to say that he was not reëngaged; nothing different could have been expected from a people who jealously guarded their children with respect to purity of Christian doctrine. Christopher Schultz was a great friend of a generous education, and, while schools were thus being conducted by the trustees, received into his family a number of Quaker boys for a time to teach them the elements of German. His own children were doubtless also pleased thus to have the chance to learn a little English.

For their benefit Schultz translated into English a short essay by Schwenkfeld on the Christian life.

On account of the small number of contributors it was agreed, 1770, that the sons of contributors to the original fund should have the right to vote if they were twenty-one years of age and should be eligible to office if they were married. Prior to 1790 the schools of the Upper or Goshenhoppen district were conducted in the private houses of Christopher Schultz, Balzer Schultz, Christopher Krauss and George Yeakel. In 1790 a combined school and meeting-house was built in Hosensack, and the following year one was built in Washington, then a part of Hereford Township, below the present Clayton. The length of school term averaged about four months per year. Prior to 1781 the teachers were not of the Schwenkfelder faith, but misunderstandings and the selfishness of some of these hirelings led the trustees to seek to employ teachers chosen from among their own people. George Kriebel and Christopher Hoffman, the ministers, both taught for a number of years, each being past fifty when he began to teach. With varied other duties pressing upon them, they thought it not beneath their dignity to enter the school-room and teach the young of their flock.

The school fund did not escape the financial misfortunes of the Revolution. In an address issued 1791, the trustees stated that by the interest of the fund of 1764 and by free contributions they supported a good school until the debtors to their fund began to pay their interest and at last the principal in depreciated currency. The debtors had received the hard-earned money of the Schwenkfelders and found it convenient and by enactment of law, legal — though not right — to repay in depreciated paper currency. This depreciation of the fund was an unfortunate, though perhaps unavoidable accompaniment of the struggle for independence. Through this shrinkage the capital stock £800 contracted to less than £100 in 1793, which was offered to the original subscribers or their heirs. Of this sum less than £12 was accepted, the rest being donated to the fund.

In 1780 the period for which the fund was originally collected expired. A general meeting of the supporters was held, at which it was agreed for the next three years to leave intact the capital which, through the accruing interest, was insufficient to meet the current expenses and which at the time was not readily convertible into specie. They divided themselves into four classes to be taxed pro rata under given conditions to meet the running expenses. An inspector was also elected to supervise the schools, and it was agreed that no child should be allowed to attend school that did not know the alphabet. This plan of dividing the supporters into classes and of thus paying the teachers, etc., was continued until 1823, when the original plan of the schools was superseded by other methods. The fund amounting to about £146 became the nucleus of the literary fund as it exists to-day which is considered in a different connection.

This school system reached its highest efficiency during 1790–92 under the instruction of George Carl Stock, who afterwards served as a Lutheran minister. In August, 1790, an agreement was entered into by the trustees with George Carl Stock, of Halle, as teacher in Goshenhoppen for one year at £5 ($13.33) per month with free dwelling and fire-wood. This may seem a low salary but it must be remembered that George Kriebel, a minister, a large landholder and a man of means taught for half this salary. Stock agreed to teach English, German, Latin, Greek, etc.

Joachim Langens
Verbesserte und Erleichterte
Lateinische
GRAMMATICA,
mit einem
Paradigmatischen und Dialogischen
TIROCINIO.
Fünf und zwanzigste Edition,
Mit stehend bleibenden Schriften
aber
um mehrerer Richtigkeit willen
Die Fünfte.

CVM PRIVILEGIIS
Sacr. Cæf. Maiestatis, Regum Poloni= ae Borußiæ,
nec non Electorum Saxoniæ er Brandenburg.

HALLE
In Verlegung des Wäysenhauses,
1741.

Ein
wohl eingerichtetes deutsches
A B C=
Buchstabir= und Lesebuch
zum Gebrauch
deutscher Schulen.
Enthaltend.
Das A B C, nebst vielen Arten Buchstabir= und Lese=
übungen. Eine Anweisung das Deutsche recht zu ler=
nen, mit einem kurzen Unterricht vom Schreiben
und Rechnen.

Etliche angenehme und lehrreiche Erzählungen, Fabeln mit Ku=
pfern, und poetische Stücke.

Eine kurze Erdbeschreibung, und ein sinnreiches Bild vor dem
Buche.

Germantaun
Gedruckt bey Michael Billmeyer, 1795.

INAUGURAL

Botanico-Medical Dissertation,

ON THE

Phytolacca Decandra

OF

LINNÆUS.

By BENJAMIN SHULTZ,
OF PENNSYLVANIA,
MEMBER OF THE PHILADELPHIA MEDICAL SOCIETY.

PHILADELPHIA,
PRINTED BY THOMAS DOBSON,
AT THE STONE-HOUSE, №. 41, SOUTH SECOND-STREET
1795.

SELECTÆ

E VETERI

TESTAMENTO

HISTORIÆ.

Ad usum Eorum qui Latinæ Linguæ Ru=
dimentis imbuantur.

NOVA EDITIO,

PRIORIBUS MULTO EMENDATIOR.

◊◊◊◊◊◊◊◊◊◊

PHILADELPHIÆ

Excuderunt PRICHARD et HALL, vico vulgariter dicto Market
Street, et J. JAMES, vico Chesnut Street

M.DCC.LXXXI.

SCHOOL BOOKS USED IN THE SCHWENKFELDER SCHOOLS, ALSO DR.
BENJAMIN SCHULTZ'S THESIS ON THE POKE-WEED.

He opened the school which he was wont to call "Our Academy," September 1, 1790, where the present Schwenkfelder meeting house in Hosensack stands in the new school-house just erected and which was replaced by a new house in 1838. The school was continued without intermission seemingly for the year, when the contract was renewed for another year, but for some unexplained reason the school was closed at the end of April, 1792.

The following words are quoted from a circular letter dated, "Philadelphia County, March, 1791," and will furnish some interesting data. The trustees "have lately and at their own expense erected a new school-house and dwelling-house for its master and engaged a man of good learning and fair character to be the master of that school in which children of parents of any religious denomination, English or German, rich or poor, may be taught reading, writing, cyphering and some or other young men of genius instructed in mathematics and the learned languages and trained up to become ushers or assistants to this or any other school in this country. Catechisms and other doctrinal books of any religious school shall not be introduced in this school. Parents may form the minds of their children in their own way or may commit them to the clergy of the church or meeting to which they belong. The master of the school shall nevertheless use his utmost endeavors to impress on their tender minds the fear of God, the love of their country and of all mankind. This well-meant school is undertaken by a few persons of but moderate estates on whom the expense of supporting and improving it will fall very heavily. The trustees flatter themselves with the hope that it will meet with some encouragement from the benevolent who have the good of the growing youth of this country at heart by contributing their mite towards this purpose."

Unfortunately the school roll has not been located and may have been destroyed. From the treasurer's accounts it is evident that children of non-Schwenkfelder families attended: Isaac Schultz, John Schultz, Jacob Yeakel, Susanna Yeakel are known to have attended. John Krauss, Christopher Yeakel, David Yeakel and Andrew Yeakel, the sons of Balthasar, probably attended, although there is no positive evidence available at the time of writing.

Among the books known to have been used are the following: *Cornelii Nepotes, Schrevelius' Greek and Latin Lexicon, Sheridan's English Dictionary, Guthrie's Geographical and Historical Grammar, Gesner's Latin and German Lexicon, Latin Selections from the Old Testament,* also two globes, a terrestrial and a celestial, with a treatise on the same by Adams. That the students studied Latin and Greek is known from direct testimony to that effect and from the Latin letters written by them still extant. Nor were these Latin letters epistles of love full of soft sentimentalities and glittering generalities. They propounded and answered questions bearing on the Bible, its doctrines, etc. The teacher also dictated to his pupils a series of propositions bearing on revealed theology that were written out in full, among others, by Susanna Yeakel, probably the daughter of Melchior, a farmer's girl of fifteen. Of these propositions, 28 treated of the Bible in general, 34 of God, 25 of the Trinity, 9 of creation, 10 of Providence, 7 of angels.

In the afternoon of New Year's day, 1791, the teacher read a paper, practically a sermon, based on 2 Cor. VI. 2 in the school-house before his pupils, patrons and others. The original, still preserved, suggests a careful, conscientious, methodical and God-fearing man. In concluding his remarks he spoke directly to his pupils and ended as follows: "The Lord grant that through my teaching you may be trained to become useful members of human society on earth and what is most important to become members of the army of the redeemed in the unending eternity beyond. According to man's expectations and the course of nature I shall probably pass beyond the grave long years before you. What a joy it will be, my dear children, to see you before the throne of God when your brief course is run and before the seat of the Lamb that was slain, to join with you in the new song: Holy, holy, holy Father, Son and Holy Spirit, Amen, So let it be."

Shortly before the Hosensack Academy was finally closed in April, 1792, George Kriebel, the pastor, paid a visit to it and addressed the scholars in a quasi-Baccalaureate sermon. The line of thought is indicated by the following brief outline gathered from his own fuller notes: Worthy and beloved young people and in particular the linguists: In view of the probability that the present school may before long be brought to a close, I have concluded to present a few matters briefly to you.

1. The consciousness that the school was made a possibility and a reality through sacrifice by members of our small religious body in the hope that you might be trained to become useful in various relations should make you circumspect in your conduct lest discouragement be produced among those who aided the cause.

2. It will at all times be pleasing to God and helpful to you to say with Samuel: "Speak, Lord! thy servant heareth."

3. In choosing a profession, strive not to have days of ease, or to avoid heavy toil, or to win glory and honor; rather say with David: "Shew me thy ways, O Lord;

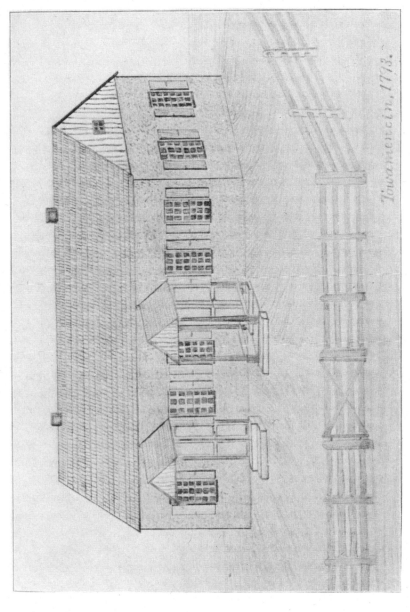

THE PENNSYLVANIA-GERMAN SOCIETY.

Towamencin, 1773.

TOWAMENCING MEETING HOUSE IN 1793.

(FROM AN OLD PENCIL SKETCH.)

teach me thy paths. Lead me in thy truth and teach me; for thou art the God of my salvation; on thee do I wait all the day." Ps. XXV. 4, 5.

4. Do not allow your knowledge to make you vainglorious or proud. Be humble and seek to be serviceable.

5. Stand by our religious society or rock from which you have sprung. Do not abuse what you have received.

6. Avoid all heathen writings and read useful and edifying books, in particular the New Testament and the writings of Casper Schwenkfeld.

When the school system of their own was abandoned by the Schwenkfelders, they joined in with their neighbors in educational efforts. Upon the adoption of the public school system some of them feared the abridgment of personal liberty and the secularization of the schools, but they became its friends and have continued its friends ever since. The whole life shows that as a body they were close friends of education at all times. Isaac Schultz doubtless gave a fair presentation of them when he wrote in 1844: "They pay great attention to education, to the religious and moral training of their children. Many of them possess a respectable knowledge of the learned languages, Latin, etc. There is scarcely a family among them that does not possess a well-selected and neatly arranged library among which you will find manuscript copies from their learned fathers." It must not be overlooked that some were opposed to schools and did not take kindly to an advanced education.

A revival of interest in education by the Schwenkfelders as a body has manifested itself in recent years. Accordingly their General Conference in October, 1891, appointed a committee of seven members to take into consideration the advisability of establishing a school for advanced or secondary education. The outcome was that "Perkiomen Seminary" was organized and put into active operation at Pennsburg, Pa., in the fall of 1892 under the principalship of Reverend Oscar Schultz Kriebel. In its ten years' existence it has risen to the front rank among private secondary schools of the state and has amply repaid itself in the work accomplished. To quote from a recent catalogue :

"It is the aim of the school to furnish our worthy young people the very best possible educational advantages for the least possible expense. The founders of the school who gave so liberally of their thought and means are Christian men and women who believe in the necessity of a thorough and symmetrical development of all the powers of mind and body for the greatest usefulness and service in life. It is the purpose of the management to carry out the idea of the founders in such a way that the young people who attend the school may receive such thorough training, such wholesome development, and such wise and careful direction of their powers and activities as will fit them in the best possible manner for the exacting requirements of a higher course of training or the actual responsibilities of life."

A RELIC OF BY-GONE DAYS.

CHAPTER X.

The Schwenkfelders as Citizens.

NDER this chapter will be considered the Schwenkfelders in their relation to the government, and more particularly with respect to the question of bearing arms. In doing this it will be proper to take a preview by stating that they were professing adherents of the views of Schwenkfeld even with respect to this relation in life. They, therefore, believed in following the "Golden Rule" even in the management of the civil affairs of life. They believed that the spirit directing and moulding the conduct of men towards their fellows should be the spirit of intercession, edification, service, peace, patience, forgiveness, humility, kindness, truthfulness and justice. They believed in the right of free speech and did not hesitate to express themselves when occasion seemed to suggest a necessity. They did not regard it incompatible with the professions of a Christian to hold office, neither did they deem it necessary for a public officer to be a professing Christian. They did not strive for public office, since they preferred the freedom of private life; neither did they in general refuse to serve when called upon. It was with them a matter of religious faith to be obedient to those in authority, and they always did obey when matters of conscience did not enter into the question. They were opposed to war and oaths and dared to stand true to their convictions, even though the community and the State were set against them and made them suffer for their fidelity to their consciences. A study of the details of their history will substantiate these statements, but as space will permit no more, a few illustrative instances only can be referred to.

Their pledge of allegiance, noticed in a different connection, was honestly made and honestly kept. In pursuance of an " act for naturalizing such foreign Protestants as are settled or shall be settled in any of the colonies," a company of Schwenkfelders took and subscribed the qualifications for them appointed by said act before John Kinsey, Thomas Graeme and William Till, judges of the said court in April, 1743. The records show that later others took the same obligations.

The Indians were a cause of great concern to the early settlers. On this score the families among the Schwenkfelders that had moved to Macungie probably endured most hardships. Isaac Schultz says of these: "Three enterprising families, Gregorius Schultz and his two brothers-in-law, John and Balzer Yeakel, ventured in their march to cross the mountains into the so-called '*Macungier Wüstenei*,' where a few Indians and other people led a miserable existence and at times subjected them to harsh treatment. They had to endure more hardships than their friends in Goshenhoppen and the Lower District. They were occasionally put in terror by the Indians, but they found it easier to live in peace and harmony with the Indians than with their persecutors in the Old World, who had the Bible in the one hand and the sword in the other hand." In anticipation of an Indian outbreak they sold their homes and moved into the Goshenhoppen valley.

During the French and Indian War the location of the Schwenkfelders was such that they escaped the terrors of the frontier but not the burden of making defense against the Indians. Christopher Schultz wrote of this period: "In the year 1755, many war rumors arose in this and other provinces, and towards the end of the year unfriendly Indians made frequent attacks, people were killed and houses were laid desolate. It became necessary to place a heavy guard along the exposed frontier, and residents were at times called upon to come to the rescue in resisting the enemy. Our people willingly helped to bear their respective shares of the burdens that fell to the various townships without personally taking up arms against the enemy, a substitute being placed by them as their term of service came." They were subjected to some terrors, although they did not endure any special hardships.

The feeling through the Goshenhoppen valley during the summer of 1755 is shown by the following incidents. Some one made the remark that many Indians were at the house of Reverend Schneider of the Catholic mission. Philadelphia soon became alarmed at the report that there were forty Indians at one place and thirty at another. The governor sent a committee to investigate, who reported that there were Indian beggars — six warriors with wives and children, at the house of the Reverend Schneider. In the latter part of October a rumor came to Goshen-

Eine

BUSCHRIFT

an das

Volk von Neü = Engelland.

vorstellende

Di sehr große Wichtigkeit de Indianer ihrem Interesse zu
verknüpffen, nicht allein damit, daß man si gerecht und
freundlich behandele, sondern auch daß man gehörigen Fleiß
thue, das Christenthum unter ihnen zupflanzen.

Durch Samuel Hopkins, A. M. Pfarrer einer Kirch in Springfield.

Ich begreiffe daß Gott kein Annehmer der Personen ist Sondern
in jedem Volk wer ihn fürchtet, und gerechtigkeit würket, ist ihm angenehm
Apostel Petrus

Bedrükkt in Boston, 1753 Ist ein beschluß zu dem historischen Bedenk=
Buch angefügt d. Housatunnak Indianer, samt einer Nachricht
d. Methoden, welche der weyland wohls. Jo. John Sergeant,
zu fortpflanzung des Evangelii unter den besagten Indianern ge=
braucht hat

Einem anderen mendirt zur ernstlichen Betrachtung der Einwohner
von Pennsylvanien, und den andern Colonien

Philadelphia Wiederum gedrukkt bey B. Franklin und D. Hall 1757.

Aus dem Englischen also in d. Hoch=Teutsche Sprach übersetzt

SCHULTZ' TRANSLATION OF HOPKINS' ADDRESS ON THE INDIANS.

hoppen and Falckner Swamp that 1,300 French and Indians had crossed the Susquehanna at Harris' ferry and
were coming east. During the night while a heavy rain
was falling, the report was spread with such success that the
next morning a large body of men was ready to go at once
and " devour the invaders like bread " as the newspaper
of the times states it. To their mingled joy, sorrow and
disgust these brave men found out that they had been misled by an unfounded rumor. They came home, wetter,
sadder, madder men. By their shooting and shouting
they alarmed the uninformed to such an extent that they
began to flee hither and thither, passing and repassing like
bees from an upset hive until they too learned that Dame
Fame had told a tale. It was probably of this period that
Isaac Schultz wrote : " Alarm came at one time with such
force across the hills into the lower valleys of Hereford
that the residents suddenly began to prepare for flight.
They gathered their valuables; the kneading-troughs
with dough and flour in them were snatched from the
wondering bakers and with the valuables placed hurriedly
on the wagons; the fires were extinguished; the guns
were shouldered and off they started along the Maxatawny
road in the direction of Philadelphia. They stopped when
they came to the top of a hill to wait for some neighbors.
Here they were met by their old friend Christopher Schultz
when they decided to investigate the cause of the alarm.
After looking into the matter they learned that they too
had followed a false rumor."

The condition of things at this time is thus described in
Memorials of the Moravian Church, Vol. I., p. 193:
"The line of the Blue Mountains from the Delaware to
the Susquehanna became the scene of the carnival which
the exasperated savages held with torch and tomahawk

during the latter part of the winter, 1755. The defense-
less settlers were taken in a snare. They were harassed
by an unseen foe by day and by night. Some were shot
down at the plow, some were butchered at the fireside;
men, women and children were promiscuously toma-
hawked or scalped or hurried away into distant captivity
for torture or for coveted ransom. There was literally a
pillar of fire by night and a pillar of cloud by day going
up along the horizon, marking the progress of the relentless
invaders as they dealt out death and pillage and confla-
gration and drove before them in midwinter's flight hundreds of homeless wanderers who scarce knew where to
turn for safety or for succor in the swift destruction that
came upon them."

That the Schwenkfelders did their share of work thus
thrust on the more fortunate is shown by the fact that, with
others, they sent flour and other provisions to Bethlehem to
relieve distress, that Christopher Schultz and John Mack,
a Mennonite, joined in writing a strong letter of appeal for
help to their brethren in Towamencin, Christopher Weber,
Casper Kriebel, Christopher Dresher and Joseph Lukens;
that David Schultz, the surveyor, a Schwenkfelder, served
as one of the trustees of the money raised to put into the
field in April and May, 1756, "The Maxatawny and Alle-
mangle Independent Guard."

About this time the Friends began to deliberate on the
formation of "The Friendly Association for regaining
and preserving peace with the Indians by pacific measures."
The Schwenkfelders harmonizing with the principles and
purposes of the association formed a union among themselves, November 13, 1756, and subscribed £206, the interest
of which was devoted to such object. December 1, 1756,
Christopher Schultz and Casper Kriebel attended a grand

Zeigen also die Rechnungen

Daß im May und Juny 1757 zusamen gelegt worden £ 105 - 12 - 7½
und im Dec 1757 und January 1758 .. .. „ 109 - 4 - 0½
Aus dem Ganzen noch beygelegt .. .. „ „ „ „ „ 0 - 3 - 4

$$\text{Summa} \quad \overline{215 - 0 - 0}$$

So Zeigen auch die Receipts von Is.ᵉ Pemberton

Als zum ersten vom 7 Juny 1757 .. „ „ £ 105 - 12 - 0
Und zum andern vom 9 January 1758 - .. „ 109 - 8 - 0

$$\text{Summa} \quad \overline{215 - 0 - 0}$$

Wir Endesgenante bezeugen und bekennen mit dieser
unserer Unterschrift, daß wir die Rechnungen der Gelder so zu
zum vermelten Subscription gehörig sind, und laut derselbigen von uns
sämtlich an Casper Kriebel und Christoph Scholtz gezahlet worden
examinirt haben; und befinden, daß dieselbigen Gelder so wohl das
Capital Sümen als angewachsene Interesen von den besagten Casper
Kriebel und Christoph Scholtzen laut der Receipts an Israel
Pemberton, einem von den Quäkern verordneten Trustees wegen
selbiger Sache richtig angezahlet worden; Zum Zeugniß dessen
haben wir dieses eigenhändig unterschrieben an diesem
12 ten Tag January Anno 1758 ———

David Scholtze
Melchior Scholtze
Christoph Umensor
Gerhard Scholtz
Geo Schultze jun.

AUDITOR'S REPORT ON MONEY RAISED FOR "THE FRIENDLY ASSOCIA-
TION"; SHOWING ALSO HANDWRITING OF DAVID SCHULTZ,
THE SURVEYOR.

meeting of the contributors to such fund in the Friends school-house, Philadelphia. Receipts show that £105, 12, 0 was paid to the said association, June 7, 1757, and £109, 8, 0, January 9, 1758.

Concerning this effort Christopher Schultz wrote: " The Quakers as well as we and others who have scruples of conscience against taking up arms against an enemy were accused of not being willing to bear their due share of the common burdens. They took pity on the miserable condition of the inhabitants along the frontier and felt that the Indian war arose on account of the unjust treatment of the Indians and was carried on under unholy purposes to the serious detriment of the province. With these things in mind they formed a union among themselves and invited others to join them with the purpose of doing what was possible to restore peace with the Indians and to preserve the same in the future, knowing that such effort and object could only be accomplished by heavy labors and expense."

When in 1759, Conrad Weiser as agent appointed by Brigadier General Stanwix advertised for a number of wagons to carry provisions for the government to Bedford, Hereford Township responded. Melchior Shultz, Melchior Wiegner, David Meschter, Christopher Schultz, Schwenkfelders, aided — the latter as secretary and committee to go to Reading and make the contract with the agent Conrad Weiser.

From a letter by Christopher Schultz, dated December 1, 1760, we learn that after consulting friends concerning propositions made by the Friends it was agreed to contribute about half of the money raised by the Schwenkfelders towards release of poor prisoners and that the " rest could be left for further purposes, necessities and considerations." At the same time he returned also to his friend Pemberton, " Remarks on the behavior of Paupanhoal, having copied and translated the same into high Dutch."

Loving ffriend   *Philad: 9 7mo. 1757*

I have just recd. thy Letter with the Translation of Hopkin's address; I am told Finos Honor has gott it translated & printed already, but have not seen any of them, intend to write to him abt it. the Abridgment of Sergeants' Memoirs is in the press & will perpul be printed next week, when it is done I purpose to send thee some of them

Several of us intend to sett out for Easton next fourth day — how long if Business will keep us there is uncertain but I think not less than two or three weeks. I shall be glad to see thee there. I am tho' in haste Thy Real ffd.

Jos. Pemberton

LETTER FROM ISRAEL PEMBERTON TO CHRISTOPHER SCHULTZ.

In 1762, George Kriebel and Christopher Schultz were present at the Indian treaties at Easton and Lancaster.

Other treaties were probably also attended by them. There is still preserved a paper answering the question, "Why should citizens attend the treaties with the Indians," in which high ground is taken with respect to this question. Thus the Schwenkfelders in the spirit of true patriots thought and toiled and sacrificed for the general welfare. They gave an unequivocal testimony in favor of honest dealing with the red man and thus placed themselves squarely on the side of right.

The American Revolution brought perplexity, distress and many privations to the Schwenkfelders, although they as in other cases fared better than others, and comparatively speaking their lines fell in pleasant places. In approaching this period of transition we must remember the following facts: they had secured the permission of the crown of England to settle in Pennsylvania before migrating in 1734; they had promised and engaged to be faithful to the proprietor and strictly to observe the laws of the province and those of England. George Heebner and Christopher Schultz, for themselves and others, with representatives of other faiths had said in an address to Robert Hunter Morris, the Lieutenant Governor in 1754: "We know very well that we can not give sufficient thanks to the Almighty for having conveyed us into such a country, and under so mild a government where the best privileges in the known world are established." They had always sought to live as dutiful subjects should, mindful of the promises they had made. As careful and intelligent observers of the affairs of the provinces they saw the drift of things, and hoped the threatened danger and disaster might be averted. On Memorial Day, 1774, Christopher Schultz said: "The mighty ones of the British Kingdom assail our most valued liberties and we seem to be on the verge of a great change."

Parting even from an adopted parent country gave pain to them.

On the second of July, 1774, a meeting of prominent residents of Berks County was held in the Court House at Reading, which Christopher Schultz probably attended, and at which he and six others were appointed as a committee to represent the county. At this meeting the following, among other resolutions, was adopted : " That the inhabitants of this county do owe and will pay due allegiance to our rightful Sovereign, King George the Third." Five of the chosen committee, among whom was Christopher Schultz, attended a provincial meeting of deputies in Philadelphia, on the fifteenth of July, where, among other resolutions, the following was unanimously adopted : " We acknowledge ourselves and the inhabitants of this province, liege subjects of his Majesty, King George the Third, to whom they and we owe and will bear true and faithful allegiance." But the war cloud grew. In December, 1774, a county committee of observation was chosen at Reading, for Berks County, among whom was Christopher Schultz. This committee met and unanimously agreed to a proposed provincial convention, and appointed a committee of seven to represent the county, among which committee Christopher Schultz was found again. He and Melchior Wagner, a delegate from Philadelphia County, also a Schwenkfelder, attended the provincial convention for the province of Pennsylvania, in January, 1775. A series of strong resolutions was adopted, among which was the following : " Resolved, unanimously that it is the earnest wish and desire of this convention to see harmony restored between Great Britain and the colonies, * * * but if the British administration should attempt to force a submission to the late arbitrary acts of the British Parliament, in such a situation we hold it our indispensable duty to resist such force, and at every hazard to defend the rights and liberties of America." In voting for this and other resolutions, Schultz and Wagner undoubtedly represented the mind of the Schwenkfelders in general on the issues at stake.

On the nineteenth of April, 1775, the British commander at Lexington gave the word "Fire," to his soldiers, and thus by the seven deaths that resulted among the Americans, caused all the provinces to rise in arms against the mother country. In a letter to Germany, dated July 22, 1775, Christopher Schultz describes the battle of Lexington and then continues as follows: "Since the first blood was shed by the British you can not believe what a flame of war-spirit like a lightning stroke has set on fire all our provinces and caused them to glow. All are armed in full battle array. In cities even the little boys form companies and conduct military exercises. Ducking and stooping and guarding of words must be studiously practiced if great danger and the military roll are to be avoided, which latter our people have thus far escaped."

This wave of militarism and wrath must have had a tendency to hasten crystallization of sentiments bearing on the relation between England and the colonies. It brought out into still bolder relief the leading factions — those favoring and those opposing war with the mother country. Besides these two elements there was another class, numerous, respectable, divergent in minor details, who from religious motives alike were opposed to the bearing of arms — the Friends, Dunkers, Mennonites, the Schwenkfelders and others. These added another serious problem to the perplexities of those in power. The people in general could scarcely reconcile themselves to the feelings of

the " non-militants " and were often led to show their dis-
approval by acts of violence in private life, by over-offi-
ciousness in public life.   A Schwenkfelder chronicler of
the times says: " For those citizens of the province who
at the breaking out of the war did not take up arms, the
prospect was often full of fear and dread.   The mad rab-
ble said : ' If we must march to the field of battle, he who
will not take up arms must first be treated as an enemy.' "

A respectable number of inhabitants of Berks County,
who were conscientiously opposed to bearing arms held a
meeting at Reading, September 1, 1775.   In a letter
transmitting the resolutions adopted by the meeting to the
Committee of Safety in Philadelphia, William Reeser, who,
by the way, was an intimate friend of Christopher Shultz,
used these words : " Inclosed is a copy of the resolves
entered into by the deputies of a considerable number of
inhabitants of this county as are conscientiously scrupulous
of taking up arms, though at the same time fully sensible
of the justice of our cause and willing as far as in them
lies to contribute to its support. * * * I have the strongest
assurance from the numbers of the subscription that they
will ever cheerfully contribute their proportion towards the
safety and welfare of the public."   The list of delegates is
not known to their writer, neither is it possible with present
knowledge to affirm the presence or absence of Schwenkfelders, although circumstances indicate their attendance
and the resolutions certainly voiced their sentiments.

On the seventeenth of May, 1776, a day of prayer was
observed by the Schwenkfelders at the call of Congress
for such day of general prayer.   Christopher Schultz led
the services.   He read Leviticus XXVI., and by way of introduction referred to and briefly explained Amos III. 6 :
" Shall there be evil in the city and the Lord hath not

done it?" He maintained that the ministers of the English court were instruments in the hands of God like Nebuchadnezzar to punish the American people for their sins. His theme was: Seeking refuge by penitence in God the Creator, Ruler and Supporter through Christ the Lord and Protector of believers.

Space scarcely permits even a reference to the Declaration of Independence and the consequent increased pressure on the Schwenkfelders, but attention must be called to the following declaration and agreement drafted probably by Christopher Schultz and in all likelihood used as indicated, although positive proof of the latter is wanting.

A Candid Declaration of Some So-called Schwenk- felders Concerning Present Militia Affairs, May 1, 1777.

We who are known by the name Schwenkfelders hereby confess and declare that for conscience' sake it is impossible for us to take up arms and kill our fellowmen; we also believe that so far as knowledge of us goes this fact is well known concerning us.

We have hitherto been allowed by our lawmakers to enjoy this liberty of conscience.

We have felt assured of the same freedom of conscience for the future by virtue of the public resolution of Congress and our Assembly.

We will with our fellow citizens gladly and willingly bear our due share of the common civil taxes and burdens excepting the bearing of arms and weapons.

We can not in consequence of this take part in the existing militia arrangements, though we would not withdraw ourselves from any other demands of the government.

WHEREAS, at present through contempt of the manifested divine goodness and through other sins, heavy burdens, extensive disturbances by war and divers military regulations are brought forth and continued.

WHEREAS, we on the first of this month made a candid declaration concerning present military arrangements to the effect that we can not on account of conscience take part in said military affairs and

WHEREAS, it seems indeed probable that military service will be exacted from many of our people and that on refusal to render such service heavy fines will be imposed.

Therefore, the undersigned who adhere to the apostolic doctrines of the sainted Casper Schwenkfeld and who seek to maintain the same by public services and by instruction of the young have mutually agreed, and herewith united themselves to this end that they will mutually with each other bear such fines as may be imposed on account of refusal for conscience' sake to render military service in case deadly weapons are carried and used. Those on whom such burdens may fall will render a strict account to the managers of the Charity Fund in order that steps may be taken to a proper adjustment.

Coschehoppe, May 2, 1777.

A few weeks previous to this, March 31, 1777, Christopher Schultz was appointed a justice of the peace. Was this a bribe in guise to stop his mouth? It is to be regretted that no positive reliable information is at hand respecting the acceptance or non-acceptance of the commission. Non-filing of the commission in the proper county office, the absence of records by " Christopher Schultz, Justice of the Peace," silence in the various historical sketches and Schultz manuscripts and the general bearing of the Schwenkfelders towards the government in general and the Revolutionary War element in particular furnish very strong circumstantial evidence to the effect that Christopher Schultz did not accept the office.

Although great hardships had already befallen the Schwenkfelders with many others, their lot was made much more grievous by the general militia act of 1777 passed to restrain the insolence of Tories. The Pennsylvania Assembly, on the thirteenth of June, passed a stringent law which among other matters required all male white inhabitants above the age of eighteen to take and subscribe before a justice of the peace an oath in the following form: " I ——— do swear (or affirm) that I renounce and refuse all allegiance to George the Third, King of Great Britain, his heirs and successors; and that I will be faithful and bear true allegiance to the Commonwealth of Pennsylvania a free and independent State, and that I will not at any time do or cause to be done any matter or thing that will be prejudicial or injurious to the freedom and independence thereof, as declared by Congress, and also, that I will discover and make known to some one justice of the peace of said state all treasons or traitorous conspiracies which I now know or hereafter shall know to be formed against this or any of the United States of America." The law also provided that every person refusing or neglecting to take and subscribe the said oath or affirmation " shall during the time of such neglect or refusal be incapable of holding any office of place or trust in the state, serving on juries, suing for any debts, electing or being elected, buying or selling, or transferring any lands, tenements or hereditaments and shall be disarmed." The law further states that " every person who shall travel out of the county or city in which he usually resides without the certificate (of his oath) may be suspected to be a spy and to hold principles inimical to the United States and shall be taken before one of the justices who shall tender to him the oath or affirmation ánd upon refusal to take the said oath or affirmation the justice shall commit him to the common jail there to remain without bail until he shall take and subscribe the said oath or produce a certificate that he has already done so."

This "test act," as the above law was popularly known, went into operation on the first of July, 1777, and before a month had passed was used to harass the Schwenkfelders. George Kriebel, one of the number, was illegally imprisoned at Easton on charges preferred by his neighbors. On the twelfth of August, his friend Christopher Schultz drafted a strong letter to his old-time friend Sebastian Levan, of Maxatawny, who, as one of the members of the Assembly, had helped to pass the test act. On the thirteenth, Schultz went to Philadelphia to appeal to the proper authorities. He did not go in vain, for on the fifteenth of August the Supreme Executive Council took action on the case and the presumption is that George Kriebel was soon after released. The letter of Schultz is given in the Appendix. Further details are given in *Colonial Records*, XI., 269, and *Pennsylvania Archives*, V., 432 and 525. Christopher Schultz drafted a letter to his friends in Germany, December 27, 1777, from which the following words are culled: "What unrest, danger and affliction have befallen us through the fortunes of war can not well be described. * * * Rash, bold, inexperienced, conscienceless heads found means through the upheaval not only to draw the government of Pennsylvania into their own hands, but also to maintain the same, contrary to the will and mind of all people of moderation. On

account of the war all things go wrong; the demands,
injunctions and forcible extortions can scarcely be told
which continually plague those that do not blow the horn
of the war-party. Heavy fines are imposed for non-performance of military service. In spite of all this we have
not allowed ourselves to be forced into the war."

We gain a glimpse at the condition of things in connection with the celebration of Memorial Day, 1777. This
year the Schwenkfelders, contrary to custom, met at two
places simultaneously—near Palm, in Upper Hanover, and
in Towamencin. Christopher Schultz said on this occasion: "We have made use of this day for more than forty
years to meet and recall together the manifested blessings
of God and to exhort one another to gratitude, but the
period of rest seems for the present to have reached its
time of change. We have the terrible tumult of war before our ears and near our very doors. It has even come
to pass that a new law has been passed according to which
we who live in different counties do not have the right to
meet. O that we might properly benefit by these things,
confess our guilt before God, humble ourselves before Him
and move His heart to pity by a proper return with the
Prodigal Son! He surely would grant us protection as he
has shown it to us unworthy ones until now." George
Kriebel referred to this occasion in an address on Memorial Day, 1793, in which he said he regarded it one of the
most important days in their American history: "English
armies were in Philadelphia at the time and made frequent
incursions into the farming sections, occasionally quite a
distance. On account of the many reports about the army
we were uneasy about our families because in some cases
only wife and children or even only the children were at
home. We considered it, therefore, advisable to dismiss
at noon and return to our homes."

A glimpse at the general conduct and reputation of the Schwenkfelders is afforded by the following letter of George Bryan, Vice-President of the Supreme Executive Council, to Colonel John Wetzel, of Northampton, dated Lancaster, May 22, 1778: "*Sir:* The Moravians and Swenkfelders have been very urgent with Assembly to relax the Test and free them from the abjuration part. The claim of the King of Great Britain forbids anything like this being done. When that prince shall renounce his claim it will be time enough to reconsider the Test. However, as these people are not to be feared, either as to numbers or malice, it is the wish of government not to distress them by any unequal fines, or by calling them without special occasion happens, to take the oath at all. The disabilities ensuing upon their own neglect are heavy, and will without further pressing (which may be termed rigor by people in general, persecution by themselves) operate strongly upon them. On these grounds, we wish it to be understood that Council and Assembly desires to avoid any noise from these people above mentioned, and to have them dealt with as others in regard to the delinquency in the militia. Your prudent advice to your friends and deputies, without exposing these lines to the knowledge of the petitioners, will serve the public interest and oblige, Your very obed't serv't G. B." A Schwenkfelder writer says that when, in 1778, the Assembly set a day when people would either have to take the test or be forever excluded from all the rights of citizenship, the Schwenkfelders finally submitted in view of the fact that the requirement pertained only to the duties of citizenship; that it came from the power that had to give protection, and that it was a duty of every soul to be subject unto the higher powers.

Christopher Schultz penned a letter to friends in Germany, in 1779, in which he used these words: "To the glory of God we must say that His protecting hand has been over us in such a fatherly way that, notwithstanding frequent fearful prospects, urgent want, severe threats and even extortions by those in authority, it is customary for our people to say as they meet in conversation, 'no one has any reason for complaint, he ought rather to thank God who has always had ways and means of escape for us even if at times punishment befell us.' The war party has thus far not succeeded in forcing any of our people to enter the military lines although all males between 18 and 53 were enrolled in the militia classes, but exorbitant sums must be paid to escape such service." The same thoughts were repeated in a letter written in 1783 signed by a number of the leading Schwenkfelders. Space forbids further reference to other interesting material in verification of these extracts.

This does not imply that no descendants of the immigrants took arms, for we know that Balzer Heydrick was a captain, and that his brothers George and Abraham Heydrick rendered some service, but the probability is that at that time they were not taking any part in the organized religious services as conducted by the Schwenkfelders and consequently not looked upon as being part of them. Neither is it implied that Schwenkfelders did not aid the cause of freedom. In illustration of this the following by the antiquarian Abraham H. Cassel is quoted from *Historical Sketches* published by the Historical Society of Montgomery County : " George Anders, a member of the Schwenkfelder sect then living on a farm, long since known as the Meschter farm, had two very fine horses and so also had his friend and neighbor Abraham Kriebel. These, together with their handsome new wagon, just from the wheelwright, were pressed in the service of the Continental Army. Anders felt such a tender concern for his pet horses that he could hardly let them go, fearing that they might not be properly cared for. He, therefore, offered his son Abraham, then eighteen years old, to go with the horses as their groom or teamster or driver. The offer was of course gladly accepted. After he had served awhile and had gained the confidence of the superior officers he was sometimes sent considerable distances with this team for various commodities. So on one occasion he thought to take advantage of their confidence and attempted to make his escape with the team, but he dared not come home for fear of being arrested. He was therefore making his way to Goshenhoppen, in Berks County, where many Schwenkfelders lived, to his uncle, George Kriebel. But he was pursued and overtaken before he reached there, by the Superintendent of Transport. He escaped punishment by artfully pleading that he had lost his way and became so bewildered as not to know where he was. As he was yet so young and was supposed to be inexperienced about the country, the officer believed his story and therefore merely ordered him back again without any further punishment. He then served till the army was so far removed that his further services could be dispensed with. Then he got an honorable discharge, and came home with the wagon and all the horses in splendid condition."

At the organization of the society in 1782 the position of the Schwenkfelders was so well known that seemingly it was taken for granted and for many years action was but rarely taken in conferences. At the spring conference, 1828, the members took into consideration the conduct of the young people in attending the " battalions " or military parades, as contrary to the doctrines of the church, the fathers and to what Jesus Christ had taught. At the following conference it was agreed to exhort the young people of the error of their ways and to inform them that if they insisted in their course of conduct they would by their own action exclude themselves from the church and would have to be so treated — in other words expulsion from church would follow for attending military parades.

During the Rebellion, members of the Schwenkfelder church when drafted under the conscription act of Congress avoided military service by securing substitutes. In such cases the poorer members were assisted by their richer brethren.

A study of the war record of the Schwenkfelders and their descendants would seem to warrant these conclusions. (1) No one directly connected with the religious society or church of the Schwenkfelders took up arms for active service in any war since the immigration. (2) Descendants have been engaged in every war since the Revolution including the late Spanish war. (3) No Schwenkfelder ever refused to pay the fines imposed for non-performance of military service. (4) No Schwenkfelders were ever suspected of treason, toryism or disloyalty to government. (5) Less hardship befell them than most other non-combatants.

CHAPTER XI.

The Private Life of the Schwenkfelders.

O far an attempt has been made in this volume to trace the Schwenkfelders in their organized relaions. The pleasant duty remains of reviewing their private lives, their toils and sorrows. It is utterly impossible to do more than here and there to lift the curtain and thus to afford a glimpse. It will be an attempt to develop a composite picture of their ordinary past daily walk and conversation. Charity teaches us to leave the curtain down as to the many minor shortcomings and errors.

At birth, the parents would give thanks to the Father for His gift and the minister would remember mother and child in his ministrations for the people before the throne of grace. As soon as convenient thereafter a formal consecration of the child either public or private would be held. Isaac Schultz refers to this in the following words: " As soon as a child is born, a preacher or minister is called in to pray for the happiness and prosperity of the child, admonishing the parents to educate their tender off-spring; to bring them up in the nurture and admonition of the Lord, according to the will of God. Parents generally bring their little ones into the house of worship, where the same service is performed." At one time the question arose whether a minister was at liberty to render such services when the parents were not Schwenkfelders. At times some seem to have felt that this child consecration displaced baptism.

The child was early taught to offer his prayers, sing his hymns and use his pencil and book. In 1792 Rev. George Kriebel reminded the pupils of the Hosensack Academy that they had received training in Christian doctrine from their youth up. Before the child was allowed to trot away to school he was to learn his A, B, C's. As soon as able he was encouraged to copy sermons, hymns or the esteemed words of some father. This kept the child from mischief, taught him to make good use of his time and gave him a bias to what is good, true and right. He was clothed in homemade goods and not in the flimsy and delicate fabrics of the present, nor was he housed up during the winter in homes where every room registered summer heat, nor was he spoiled as to temper and digestion by gifts of cakes, sweetmeats and poisonous candies to be consumed at every unseasonable hour, nor had he a room full of tin soldiers, horses, castles, railroad trains and comic automata playthings " made in Germany."

When the child became sick or was threatened with some of the dread afflictions of childhood, domestic remedies were resorted to. Some of these were made up of herbs, roots, leaves, bark or at times their ashes. Beside these, according to a book in the hands of the writer, a record of Mrs. George Heydrick (the midwife, *d*. 1828, who notes more than 1,700 professional visits), living crabs, pulverized egg shells, skulls of dogs, the lice of sheep, worms, red beads, human hair and unwashed yarn were also deemed of medicinal value. For example, for whooping cough, take of the hair of one who never saw his father and place it around the neck of the patient, either in a bag, or sewed in the clothing or plaited into a braid; or this: give the patient bread and butter spread by one who did not change her family-name at marriage; for convulsive fits, take a skein of unwashed yarn, spun by a child under seven years of age, pass it over the forehead of the patient, then pass the patient through the skein three times the same way, burn the yarn, gather the ashes and add a little of the ashes to the patient's soup. A curious feature of modern times is to believe in somewhat similar remedies, to reject the aid of God-fearing, scientifically trained medical practitioners and to worship the faith curist.

When the child became old enough his religious training was actively entered upon. He was grounded in the fundamental principles by a study of the catechetical questions. In this study he was encouraged to write out all the proof-texts or even perhaps to commit to memory all the questions and answers of the catechism. He was taught how to understand the sacred didactic poetry found in the hymn-books or circulated in manuscript copy. He was instructed in prayer and in the duty of leading a God-fearing life. In these studies questions were often assigned to pupils in order that during their hours of toil their meditations might thus be directed. Christopher Kriebel, who had charge of the training of the young for more than thirty-three years, encouraged his pupils to write out comments on the assigned topic or Scripture passage, two weeks' time being allowed to prepare the answer. In this

Jugendlicher Handel
so
aus 142 Gedenken bestehet. wobey die
Apostel-Geschichte fragweise von
verß zu verß
durch gegangen ist

und von Zeit zu Zeit mit der

Jugend

ist abgehandelt worden
Zu Gottseliger Erbauung und Übung der Jun-
gen Gemüther, im Erkentnis Gottes u. Jesu Christi unsers Heylandes; als auch Anleitung zum Erkentnis unsers groſsen Sünden-Elendes.

und also sind allhier diese kürtze u. einfaltige Vorstellungen
dem andächtigen Leser als auch der Jugend, zur Wiederhey-
lung, Nachbetrachtung u. Prüfung gesamlet.
Zu Ende bracht 1797.
von
Chr. Krib
vierter Band.

TITLE PAGE OF THE FOURTH AND FINAL VOLUME OF NOTES ON
BIBLE STUDIES BY CHRISTOPHER KRIEBEL.

way he, for instance, spent eight years in a study of the Gospel according to St. John, his own record of the questions and answers covering more than a thousand pages of closely written manuscript.

Some of the young people were in the habit of asking each other questions concerning events, persons, etc., of the Bible — even in Latin at the time of the Hosensack Academy. At a later period the young were expected to commit to memory the gospel lessons of the whole church year and received regular drill on the same by question and answer. They copied their *Tägliches Gesang Büchlein* and thus early learned to send to Heaven on the wings of song many a petition worded in the rugged rhythms of the fathers. They copied the confessions of faith and thus fixed firmly the great truths for which the fathers suffered and fled. Although the modern Sunday-school is of recent date, the idea of imparting religious instruction on Sundays is not recent and the Schwenkfelder boy and girl have been accustomed to attend classes for religious instruction on Sunday ever since the fathers landed. Nor were these instructions limited to Sundays. Meetings were at various periods frequently held for such training during the week. Balzer Hoffman also prepared a question book on the gospel lessons covering the whole year to be used in the instruction of the young, in connection with his hymns on the same. One need not be surprised that under such intensive training, the life and thought of the young became tinged with a Pharisaic pride. The following words by one of the descendants of Christopher Schultz probably represent the feelings of others — unhappily not found alone among the Schwenkfelders : "When I first went away from home I had the idea that every denomination but the Schwenkfelders were in a

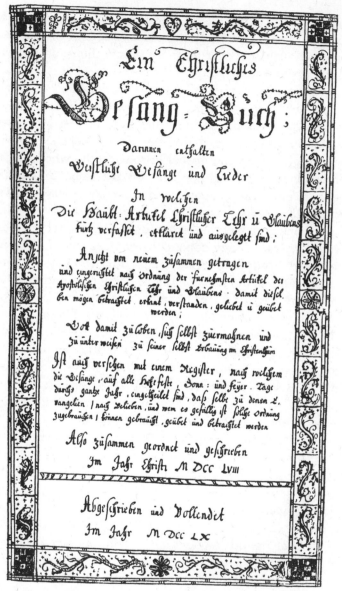

TITLE PAGE OF MANUSCRIPT SCHWENKFELDER HYMN-BOOK.

state nearly allied to the Gentiles and that it was a duty to avoid intercourse with them as much as possible. Whatever may have been the cause of this state of mind, I honestly thought that piety and morality were confined to the narrow limits of the church to which my parents belonged."

The Schwenkfelder parent was quite anxious to have his child secure at least the rudiments of the three R's. This position is well expressed in the preamble of the Agreement of 1764 quoted in another connection as follows: "The faithful training of the young in reading, writing and the study of the languages according to sex, age and standing, and their instruction in the principles of true religion contribute very much to the welfare and prosperity of every community. The boys and girls were thus sent to school and the words of Isaac Schultz fairly represent them: "They pay great attention to the education of their children." At the close of the term the teacher frequently favored them by giving them a pen-written memento, a kind of diploma or certificate of good conduct.

When the time came for the young man to think of finding a helpmate for himself, he was encouraged to seek a Schwenkfelder damsel. Fathers compared mixed marriages to a nesting together of the crow and the dove. The fathers even tried to tell him what the different steps in the selection ought to be, practically, how to pop the question, but young Cupid though blindfolded oft found ways to defeat the best laid plans of wise and pious parents and with his shafts inflicted the incurable wound. Alas! that at times the young could not see as the fathers did and later awoke to learn that they had loved neither wisely nor well. The ludicrous also happened. When young Heinrich Schneider and lovely Rosina Neuman of Gwynedd found their hearts beat as one, they started for Philadelphia to secure some proper person to declare them one. Christopher, the father, said in substance " Heinrich Schneider has stolen my Rose " and followed on horseback to prevent the impending catastrophe. His hurried ride was in vain. The twain had been wedded. God bestowed his blessing upon them and an honored patronymic was added to the list of Schwenkfelder family names. When young Christopher Schultz (afterwards the Reverend Christopher) engaged himself to Rosina Yeakel, he, as others had done, also made a will in due form bequeathing her a definite sum of money should he die before their contemplated marriage.

The following exceptional episodes are related of the courtship days of one innocent comic rural swain. He called at one place and received the " sack." On his way home either for joy or pain of heart or through a spirit of mischief, he made such a noise that the dogs along the way joined in a howling chorus and thus heralded the progress of the victim through the valleys. At another time when on a similar mission he came to a house having a so-called double-door. For some reason not explained by tradition he stepped over the lower closed half instead of opening it. One need not be surprised that he failed here too. Subsequently he called at a home where there were two buxom daughters. The older one left the room in such a manner that he had a chance to follow and make known his mission. He failed to do so and she went to bed leaving the younger sister alone with the caller. He then told her that he had called for the older sister, that although it was customary to harvest the hay before the aftermath, she would do. This meant of course another " sack."

Fourthly he tried his fortune at a place where he found a wood-chest in the sitting room. He lay down on it, saying that he found as much comfort in lying down as in sitting. Here again he failed.

When a young couple had finally decided to sail down life's stream together the next step was to go to some Justice of the Peace or church minister and have the ceremony performed. Considerable intermarrying took place. Thus the present writer can refer to 25 ancestors who came to Pennsylvania on the ship *St. Andrew* in 1734. In most cases the bridegroom, however, would go to the minister and declare their intentions in order that the same might be announced in open meeting. This was repeated several times during which period the minister met the groom and bride several times and instructed them on Christian doctrine and particularly on the duties of married life. The important day having come, the invited guests assembled at the house of the bride and awaited the minister. Regular religious services were conducted including prayer, singing and a sermon, upon which the ceremony followed and the twain were pronounced one. At the marriage feast which followed the " Schwenkfelder cake " was not missing, neither were the poor forgotten. From the table bountifully laden, the baskets were filled and members of the family dispatched to the unfortunate. Drinking, dancing and other doubtful doings were not permitted. At times the pastor would remember the new couple by sending them a letter rich with sound precepts. At one time a regulation was adopted that if members of the society were not married by the regular ministers, a confession expressive of regret at the irregular step would have to be made in open meeting Then all steps in life were regarded sacred and entrance into the married relation one of the most sacred of all.

The young bride had — perhaps for years — been making preparations for her duties as wife and mistress of the future home. She had saved the rags — in recent decades at least — and cut them into strips to be woven into carpet by father or brother. She had made the spinning wheel hum and had prepared her thread and warp and woof for her linen and linsey-woolsey. She had probably worked her samplers to ornament the spare-room, rich in a variety of colors, filled with curious shaped animals, ornamented letters and figures or perhaps even with the reproduction of bits of landscape. She had in readiness several changes of bed linen complete with quilts, comfortables and feather-bed and coverlets displaying all the colors of the rainbow arranged in designs more or less artistic. Perchance she had even started to collect her family treasure of shining pewter or queensware ornamented with letters, figures, etc. She had learned to make her own soap, to cook and bake and, what was a pride of her heart, to make a Schwenkfelder cake. This was a risen cake, spread by rolling pin, flavored by saffron, and crowned by sweetened crumbs, as wide as the oven door or baker's tools would warrant and baked in the old-fashioned bake-oven. Sad to say the fame of the cakes at times went farther than the fame of the bakers themselves. It is probable that these cakes originated in Silesia for there to this day does the busy housewife bake the same cake called *Streuselkuchen*.

It may not be amiss to take a peep at the life in the family. Isaac Schultz says in 1844 : " They — the Schwenkfelders — form a respectable part of the German community of the counties above named. Some of them pursue agriculture, some manufactures, others are engaged in commercial enterprise. By their strict discipline they keep their members orderly and pure from the contaminating influences of the corruptions so prevalent. They are a moral people; pious and highly esteemed by all who know them. They pay great attention to the education, the moral and religious training of their children. Many of them possess a respectable knowledge of the learned languages, Latin, etc. There is scarcely a family among them that does not possess a well-selected and neatly arranged library." Balzer Schultz relates the following expressions of opinion by C. E. Stock, the teacher of the Hosensack Academy, 1792 : " I must say this, of all the sects and religious bodies I have met, and they are many, I found none with whom I was so well pleased. I have now lived with you for some time and have never heard an oath or blasphemous word. I never saw one of your people drunk. You are kind and beneficent to all, particularly to the poor. You are orderly and industrious in your calling. You do not waste your substance on splendor and richness in clothing as do others. You live separated from the world and you seek to keep your children away from the world. Neither during the week much less on Sundays do you allow your children to go to places of public resort, but encourage them in the study of the Bible." Schwenkfelders were expected to pay their debts. He who did not do so, was looked upon as having forfeited the rights of membership. If a person under adverse circumstances felt the pangs of poverty gnaw at his vitals he did not need to worry about his going over the hill to the poor house, for such as these were always cared for out of the Charity Fund, at no time exhausted since its founding. Even the tramps were not forgotten and they were known to ask the way to the Schwenkfelder valley. Even the ministers had a fund placed in their hands at one time to help along the " Weary Willies " of the road.

The peculiarities of dress spoken of by some writers have passed away. Freedom was indeed guaranteed to families by church regulation, hence no particular regulations can be spoken of. New fashions, new goods, new styles were scrupulously avoided and legislated against, and as a matter of economy the use of home-made goods was encouraged.

The Schwenkfelders were not office seekers though when called upon they usually served. Christopher Schultz was commissioned as a Justice of the Peace in 1777 but in all probability failed to accept the commission. Christopher Hoffman was appealed to by messengers to serve in a certain office for which he had been chosen but flatly refused. After the messengers had left, he said to his wife: " Oh how good is it to be able to remain humble." A few years after this Abraham Schultz was a member of the Pennsylvania Assembly and as such served on various committees. In more recent times the Schwenkfelders have drifted more towards public office. They have, however, always been close students of public affairs and have been intelligent readers of the current secular and religious papers. Nor have they hesitated to express themselves when occasion seemed to demand. They have always been law-abiding. They were averse to resorting to law although ready even thus to maintain their rights, if need be.

The Schwenkfelder farmer was not averse to having redemptioners in his household. Abraham Beyer, Andrew Beyer, David Schultz and Christopher K. Schultz are known to have employed them. In the case of David Schultz, Hans Ulrich Seiler had originally been helped by Abraham Beyer the father of Mrs. David Shultz who paid his ship-passage from Rotterdam. He was of a very

ugly and surly disposition. To improve matters surveyor
David took the German into his own household. The outcome was that Mrs. Schultz was cruelly murdered, June
14, 1750, by Seiler, who after due process of law was executed the following November, the first German to be executed in Pennsylvania according to David Schultz. They
probably never were negro slaveholders, but they are not
known to have offered any assistance to the underground

RECEIPT GIVEN BY REV. H. BIBIGHAUS FOR $273.02, RAISED BY THE SCHWENKFELD-
ERS FOR THE USE OF THE REV. BENJAMIN SCHNEIDER, D.D., MISSIONARY OF THE RE-
FORMED CHURCH AT BROOSA IN ASIA MINOR. (See page 93.)

railroad. When the president or the governor called for a
day of prayer, humiliation or thanksgiving the Schwenkfelders, as all loyal citizens heartily responded. Nor did
he deem it too much trouble to go forty miles to cast his
vote at a Provincial election.

In their secular employments they were mostly farmers though many served their fellows in various other

capacities.   The peripatetic shoemaker, tailor, nailmaker, fencemaker were well known.   The various steps in the manufacture of linen goods from the sowing of the flax-seed in the well-manured and well-cultivated garden spot to the bleaching or dyeing of the fabrics by home-made dyes was well-known to them by actual experience.   In harvest time the larger farmers would have half a dozen grain-cradles or more in their fields which meant the employment, feeding and lodging of perhaps a score of extra hands. David Schultz, surveyor, remarks in his diary that he employed twenty-four reapers one day.   With five or six, or seven meals a day of good substantial food, a demijohn of applejack on the pump floor and perhaps one in the field, a great amount of work would be done.   How they would rejoice at the familiar long drawn sound of the dinner horn possibly tooted by a mischievous youngster sitting on the houseroof.   If at night strange noises or merry laughter were heard, or beds turned upside down, or wagon wheels misplaced, or dead chickens placed on long poles in front of the open bedroom windows none was the wiser or less agreeable in the morning.

In turning his products into cash, the Schwenkfelder farmers would haul the grain to Flourtown, Germantown or Philadelphia.   With his neighbors he would organize butter market companies in order that each of the half dozen or more farmers might take his turn in going to the "town."   He would start in the small hours of the morning, with four horses attached to his heavy laden Conestoga wagon, with possibly a couple of the daughters occupying the front seats who hoped to see the sights and make purchases for the family.   Such rides on a springless Conestoga over the rocks, around the stumps, on uncushioned boards with thrusts against the sides of the wagon-body must have caused a voracious appetite and the most charming rosy cheeks and dimpled chins. The day's journey ended, the team would probably follow a long train of similar wagons to one of the numerous hostleries along the road, and the wants of man and beast would be attended to for the night. Going to bed meant for the teamsters then, lying on a bag of feed on the floor of the bar-room, trying to sleep, telling his tale of woe, listening to blood-curdling stories or cracking his jokes, sometimes rather coarse. Thus he went. On his return trip he would bring salt for his stock, gypsum for his fields, fish for the family and neighbors, storegoods for the country merchant, and last but not least by any means in the estimation of the recipients, trinkets for the little boys and girls in exchange for the nuts or nicely combed hog bristles given him to market. Tradition tells us that where East Greenville is now located there was formerly one of the worst stretches of road along the whole Philadelphia route, one that farmers always dreaded — and particularly on cloudy, moonless nights — the winding between the trees and through the bogs and low places axle-deep with sticky mud.

When the apples were ripe, apple butter parties were in order. Who can declare the rural joy in picking apples under the wide spreading apple trees and making the luscious cider at the old-fashioned home-made cider mill, in drinking the sweet cider or eating the rich cidersoup, in making bushels of " schnitz," in stirring the mixture of schnitz and cider until the proper consistency has been reached, in trying to eat the tempting fool cake filled with tow prepared by the smiling, haughty farmer's daughter, in dipping the finished product from the copper kettle and gathering up the remains along the sides of the kettle either with crooked finger or crust of bread and eating to one's heart's content. He who has not joined on such or similar occasions in playing a game of " Blumsock " (hunt the slipper) knows not what genuine innocent sport is.

At times spinning wheels would be shouldered, and a visit made to a neighbor to talk and spin. The years crops being all harvested, thrashing was in order which was done by flail, or rude machine or the quasi-Scriptural method of letting the horse tread out the golden grain. If there was naught else to do, spinning was engaged in by father, mother, son and daughter the whole winter through, the aim being to finish the year's spinning by Candlemas — " *Lichtmes. Spin Vergess.*" Some might occasionally be seen working on the tape machines weaving strings, either ornamental for the Sunday-go-to-meeting apron or plain for household use or for father's grain bags. The various looms too were kept in motion and the miller in the hollow sang and whistled as his wheel turned round, grinding out the grist or yielding the pure linseed oil and meal.

When the snows began to fall and sleighing was thus assured, Christoffel or Balthasar or Hans Heinrich would sniff the air, and say to Bevvy and Molly, " To-night we will take a sleigh ride." Word would be sent to the neighboring houses, the home-made bob-sleigh would be brought forth, the wagon body placed on it and half filled with clean straw. Grain bags would be stuffed full of straw and placed cross-wise for seats. In due time eight, ten or a dozen pairs of the neighboring boys and girls would start off. The inexperienced can not appreciate the pleasures of a sleigh ride in a crisp, moonlight night, horses prancing, sleighbells ringing in bright jingling tones, girls, laughing, dogs barking, the hills reëchoing, and all hearts light and gay and free. The spacious farmhouse of some blood relation or friend being reached, all would jump out,

WEAVING TAPE ON A HEDDLE LOOM.

A SCHWENKFELDER MUSIC BOOK.

some perhaps to measure their own length in a snowdrift, the horses would be led to the spare stalls back of the cows, and the good wife would make the whole company feel welcome. Games were perhaps indulged in, but none such as might prove but nurseries of future wrong-doing were allowable. Supper was served and as the small hours of the morning came the company broke up and the rustic lads and lasses wended their way homeward.

In his religious life the Schwenkfelder would begin and end each day in prayer, though oft in secret and inaudibly. At each meal, either silently or audibly, by prayer, song or the innocent child's lisping, he would return thanks to God for his gifts. He had his book of daily prayers and hymns, which he did not fail to use. If he wished to have a particular book, either in manuscript or print, he did not regard it beneath his dignity, or as unworthy of his manhood, or as being a useless waste of time, to copy such envied production in full for himself. He would even take up knotty questions in theology for study and write out his comments. In his library he had the sermons, either printed or written, of Werner, Hiller, Weichenhan Hoburg, the Epistolaren of Schwenkfeld, the mystic writings of Hoburg and the collections of letters of more recent times. These he read and studied. He had courses of reading so that various books might be read through in course during the year. The Pennsylvania Historical Society, has one of these " courses " complete for the church year, in which all the leading Schwenkfelder writers, from Schwenkfeld to Balzer Hoffman, are referred to. Each Sunday has readings arranged for *Früh*, *Vormittags*, *Nachmittags*, *Kinderlehr*. The authorship is not determined. On Sunday, if he did not go to meeting, he would have his devotions in his home. After the morning chores were done and the family clothed in the clean home-spun to be worn the following week, the family would gather, hymns were sung, prayers offered, perhaps read out of his book of prayers, and the sermon for the Sunday read by some one of the family. Woe to the child that fell asleep. If a hearer became listless, the book would be passed to him with a request to continue the reading. Doubtless the minds of the youthful worshippers would be wandering over the green pastures, beside the still waters or by the shady swimming pool, while the body was paying due respect to the solemnities of the occasion. Sermon ended, the dinner and the feeding of the lowing herd would demand attention. In the afternoon the young would not be allowed to wander away from home to engage in mischief. They would gather for instruction in their places of worship, or, staying at home, would copy sacred hyms or sermons, or engage in other religious exercises, or as amateur artists they would paint houses, ornamental letters, or creations of the imagination; betimes the young ladies of the household would ply their needles on their fancy work. Before 1790 the Schwenkfelder had no house of worship to go to. When after that he went to his place of prayer and praise he had no bell to call the people, no backs or cushions to the seats, no stained glass windows, no carpets to hush the footfall of the belated worshipper, no ushers to tell the people to come up higher, no organ to drown the voice of the singers, no choirs to praise God by proxy, no Rev. Blank, D.D., LL.D., to dazzle with a sensational pyrotechnic display of smooth-flowing cadences and glittering generalities. The service he attended was non-liturgical though the sermon or prayers were occasionally read from printed books or from manuscripts. His preacher served without pay, hence could be fearless and free and had no occasion to measure the effect of his labors by the subscriptions in the successive collection books.   In worship sexes and ages were seated separately, men were dressed so much alike that one would involuntarily think of uniforms.   The snow-white caps, aprons and neckerchiefs of the women placed the worshipper in a devotional frame of mind.   The boys and girls sat by the parents in their home-spuns and probably barefooted in summer time.   In prayer they stood in reverent attitude, and as the names of the Saviour were mentioned by the preacher they all slightly bent the knee, and thus visibly and inaudibly expressed their amens to praise and supplication.

As an illustration of the procedure when death invaded the family and claimed a victim we will quote Christopher Kriebel's letter of 1769: "We in 'Coschehoppe, Shippach and Towamencin,' have our own burying grounds at each place.   Many have burying grounds on their own land for their families.   Others who lived a considerable distance away have buried their dead in burying grounds of people who are not of our faith, since those of quite different religious views have buried there for the earth is quite common to such use in our land.   We have also allowed our neighbors who live near us and are of different religious views to bury in our grounds.   The ceremony with us is as follows: on the death of any one, there is a general consultation between the family of the deceased and the neighbors in reference to the burial of the body; a duty is assigned to each one which he is expected to attend to until the ceremonies are ended.   At the same time provision is made for messengers to go on horseback to the distant places where our people reside, and since for a long time no minister has been among us, a request is made at the

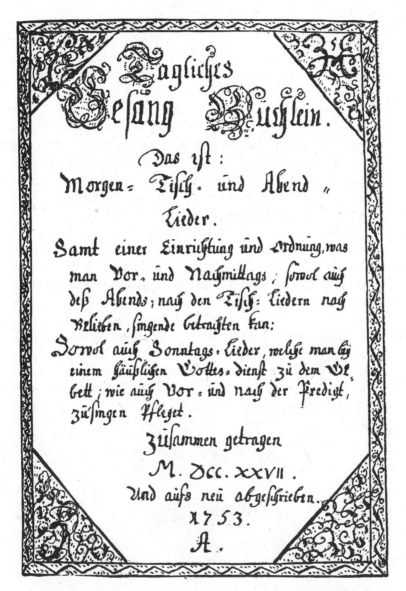

TITLE PAGE OF MSS. HYMN BOOK FOR FAMILY WORSHIP.

same time of the one who is to speak a word of exhortation on the occasion of the funeral. On account of our homes being considerably scattered many horses are brought together (the women are as good riders on their side-saddles as the men; there is no difference). The horses from a distance are fed, the people are provided with bread, butter and a refreshing drink, on cold days warm drinks are provided. The care of horse and man, the digging of the grave and the burial are entrusted to the neighbors who are designated by the bereaved family. The place where the preaching takes place is at times under the open sky, but mostly in the barns which usually prove entirely too small, so that many have to sit and stand outside. The exercises are opened with the singing of a hymn or two, which is followed by a discourse of perhaps an hour and a half and then closed by another hymn. Upon this the body is carried to the grave and buried while a hymn is sung. Thanks are expressed for the love shown during the bereavement and invitations are given to return to the house of mourning for refreshment." Though reforms and changes have been introduced in funeral customs, the essential mode of procedure has not been materially changed, since this was written.

CHAPTER XII.

HE preface of the second edition of
the *Catechism* by Christopher Schultz
opens with these words : " A pure,
Christian system of doctrine of faith
is among all temporal gifts and
favors of God, the greatest and
most important." In these words
the author but voices the controlling
sentiment of all sincere and earnest
Schwenkfelders. Among such people, the student would
naturally expect to find in addition to doctrinal education,
considerable activity in the line of religious literature and
such has been the case. Casual reference has been made
to this in earlier chapters ; an effort will be made to present a concise review of the American efforts in this direction without attempting to catalogue all the productions.

The correspondence of these people with their European
friends and acquaintances affords much light in this direction. This began probably as early as 1731 when George
Schultz, the brother of surveyor David, landed in Philadelphia. The present writer has in this connection com-

piled a partial list of over 200 letters still preserved extending from 1733 to 1792, some of which are quite lengthy
productions.   It is probable that prior to 1765 the correspondence was somewhat limited partly due to the fact that
means of conveyance or the mail facilities were meager.
At that time, however, on account of Heintze, Kurtz, Groh,
Fliegner and others, living in or near Probsthayn, more
interest began to manifest itself.   Thus for instance we
read that in 1769, 39 letters were enclosed in one package,
in 1770, 41, and in 1774, 44.[1]   From 1776 to 1784, there
was almost a complete interruption of correspondence on
account of the Revolutionary war.   These letters are a mine
of information respecting the inner life of the community
during the whole period.   A package of them was found
by Ober-Lehrer Friedrich Schneider in his extensive historic researches who wrote these words in reference to
them : "From all of these there shines forth a pious and
peaceful mind.   The condition of these Schwenkfelders
is continually good.   In expression most of these letters
are correct, fluent and cultured. * * * The letters of this
Susanna Wiegner (Mrs. George Wiegner) in spite of her
age are written in a firm and neat hand and their style
betrays an unusual education."   In subject matter these
were letters of friendship, business, religious exhortation
or doctrinal controversy of an individual or general nature.   From this correspondence we also learn that efforts
were made at various times by the Schwenkfelders to rescue their old doctrinal books, among others those taken
from them during the time of the Jesuit Mission 1720 to
1726.   Considerably prior to 1767, boxes full of books

---

[1] Sample "addresses" of these letters : "Aan Monsier George Hübner in
Pencilvania im Valckner Swam"; "Aan Melchior Hübner 12 Stonden von
Philadelphia in Pensilvania " ; "Dises Briflein zu kommen an George Hübner
als meinem liben Schwager in Pensilvanien."

SCHWENKFELDER MATRONS.

DRESSED FOR PUBLIC WORSHIP AS CUSTOMARY DURING LAST CENTURY.

were imported through their friend Wigand of Frankfort. The price of an Epistolar of Schwenkfeld was 12 to 18 gulden—a gulden equals 41 to 48 cents. References show that other importations were made and that money was raised for such purpose.

Besides this correspondence the early life in Pennsylvania shows remarkable activity in denominational literature. Many of the manuscript volumes are still preserved and prove rich feasts to the eye of the book-lover. Numbers of these have been allowed to pass into strange hands to be highly treasured or to be allowed to be destroyed. Some of the volumes are stately developments of lines of thought more or less profound; others mere collections of papers on allied themes; others, record of work in the training of the young; others, crude "Whatnots" for the preservation of literary gems or curiosities. Series of sermon outlines by most of the ministers are still preserved affording much valuable information. Writings of a controversial nature are not wanting either as for instance those against the views of Jane Leade, or Jacob Boehme, or the restorationists or the lively sparring of Joshua Schultz and Daniel Weiser.

With respect to a special line of work, Hon. S. W. Pennypacker used these words in an address before the Pennsylvania-German Society: "I want to call your attention to another sect, the Schwenkfelders who came to Pennsylvania. They were the followers of Casper Schwenkfeld and the doctrines taught by him were almost identical with those taught by the Quakers. They came in 1734. Their literature was extensive and interesting. It is reproduced for the most part in huge folios written upon paper made at the Rittenhouse paper-mill on the Wissahickon, the earliest in America. These volumes sometimes contained 1000 pages, bound in stamped leather with brass covers and brass mounting. (Christopher Hoffman was their bookbinder. H. W. K.) Among the notable facts connected with their history is that they prepared a written description of all the writings of Schwenkfeld and their other authors and it is as far as I know the first attempt at a bibliography in this country." (*Pennsylvania Germans*, Vol. II., 38.) In connection with this bibliography a record was made of the contents of the books owned by the different families (1741–1747) in the Salford and Towamencin districts. The abrupt breaking off of the record suggests the probability that it had been planned to extend the list. The writer has no knowledge that anything like this was attempted since.

It is worthy of note that the huge manuscript volumes were in nearly every instance supplied with registers or indexes. Too often, it is to be feared, people have looked upon these manuscript volumes as a quantity of paper rather than as a record of midnight toil and anguish of soul, historic accretions of profound thinking, rubies and diamonds perchance for the adornment of God's spiritual temple and kingdom. Fortunes have been won and lost but no one seems to have thought of collecting, collating and saving from destruction, these treasures by providing a place for them and a fund for their proper care, study and publication. Can God bless a people that carelessly despises its heritage and forgets its history?

It will be profitable and instructive to particularize a little more closely with respect to the work done by some of these toilers.

George Weiss, son of Casper, was born in Harpersdorf, Lower Silesia, Germany, in 1687. Abandoning his property on account of persecution, he like others went with his family to Saxony in 1726 and to Pennsylvania in 1734, where he died in 1740. As a youth he was not allowed to be idle if one may judge by his copying Michael Hiller's *Postill* before he was thirteen years old. His father, a strenuous Schwenkfelder, collated a large hymn-book, a large book of prayers, and glosses or comments on various passages of the Bible. The son in helping to copy these, early received a sound religious training. In 1720 George wrote a *Confession of Faith* for the Schwenkfelders and answers to the questions propounded by the Jesuit missionaries. About the same time he wrote an extended article on clothing in which he took a very stringent position in favor of simplicity of dress and against the innovations creeping in on the Schwenkfelders. By 1730 he had completed a series of poetic productions collected in a volume having the following title page literally translated : "*Meditations, that is studies and spiritual explanations of the names of different patriarchs and prophets in the Old Testament and of the evangelists and apostles in the New Testament with expositions of the hidden mysteries bearing on Christ the Son of God who was to and did assume flesh and in it did redeem his people and unite man with God; composed, meditated and arranged in simple rhyme according to the mind (Sinn) of the Holy Spirit and the Holy Scriptures.*" About the same time he practically rewrote Suderman's hymns based on the Song of Solomon rearranging the same, assigning a suitable melody and in many cases adding one or more stanzas. In 1733, he began to write letters to various members of the Schwenkfelder community on Scripture passages as a means of religious culture and thus in a little more than a year composed material that would fill almost 400 pages of a book octavo size. After the migration to Pennsylvania he continued this doctrinal and devotional letter writing. At death he left incomplete several series of studies in the line of revealed theology, and about 1,600 catechetical questions on creation, prayer, the Lord's Prayer, faith, the Ten Commandments, the Christian church, the knowledge of Christ, Baptism, the Lord's Supper and marriage.

Balzer Hoffman, like his bosom friend George Weiss, was born in Harpersdorf, 1687, and under like circumstances came to Pennsylvania, where he died in 1775. The importance of his father Christopher is indicated by his being chosen as one of the three Schwenkfelders to go to Vienna to plead tolerance before Charles VI. Like Weiss, young Balthasar also copied his *Postill* before he was thirteen years old. During the Vienna mission he as one of the three aided in placing seventeen memorials before Charles. His son Christopher made out a descriptive catalogue of his writings, the original of which is in the possession of Hon. S. W. Pennypacker. According to said catalogue, the period of his productive writing extends at least from 1722 to 1773. The catalogue enumerates 58 tracts, refers to 83 letters and fails to mention his hymns, his historical sketches and minor productions. The writings are classified under three heads : (*a*) *Studies of the Bible either by verses or chapters; (b) other useful studies and confessions,* and (*c*) *studies of hymns.* Want of space forbids enumeration of these. Among the more important efforts are the following :

1722. A short catechism.

1724. A postill called *Epistasia* on the Epistle lessons of the church year. He arranged the same texts in rhymes 1726 and composed prayers to accompany them 1738.

1725. A study of the epistle to the Hebrews called *Hexatomus.*

1734. A postill on the gospel lessons for the church year called, *Evangelische Jahr Betrachtung*. He prepared questions as a guide for the study of these in 1744 and also arranged them in rhyme.

1743. A glossary in German of Scripture terms.

1751. A careful study of the Apostle's Creed.

He composed studies of many hymns, wrote out in comparative fullness his "Gedächtniss tag" sermons, prepared historical sketches of the Schwenkfelders and worked out elaborate productions in the line of revealed theology. One of these was called *Hodophænum*. He seems to have supervised the copying of the Weiss hymn-book by his son Christopher, and thus performed serviceable work preliminary to the hymn-book of 1762. Before the migration, he at various times, quaintly used the pseudonym, *Barachiah Heber* or implied his initials *B. H.* by placing prominently on the title page two words beginning with these letters.

Christopher Schultz, son of Melchior, was born in Harpersdorf, 1718, was taken to Saxony by his parents at the time of their flight, came as an orphan to Pennsylvania and died in 1789. He was a remarkable man and for many years the chief figure in the Schwenkfelder community. He was all his life a close student, a clear thinker, and a fearless, Godfearing Christian. With respect to his literary work the following cursory remarks at least seem in place. His description of the voyage to Pennsylvania in 1734 by the Schwenkfelders is a classic in its way, and does credit to an orphan of sixteen. He collected some of the letters of George Weiss and probably his catechetical questions also about the year 1743. He copied Hoffman's *Hexatomus*, 1746, and probably aided in the preparation of a paper on marriage with respect to views and customs among the Schwenkfelders, 1748. From 1750 to 1775 he wrote the *Historische Anmerckungen*, published in the *Americana Germana*, Volume II., No. 1. From a letter to his friend Israel Pemberton the following words are quoted : " With these presents I do return the remarks on the behavior of Paupanahoal, having copied and translated the same into high Dutch. It hath been very acceptable to several of my friends who rejoice in perceiving the hand of grace to operate so strongly on the poor heathen." In the publication of the *Neu-Eingerichtetes Gesangbuch* of 1762 he was a hearty worker. In 1763 the first edition of his *Catechism* was issued. In 1764 he led the Schwenkfelders in organizing the school system described in another chapter. In 1768 he prepared a short sketch of Schwenkfeld and his followers at the request of his friends, Anthony Benezet and Israel Pemberton, which with other material was sent to the Queen of England, Charlotte of Mecklenburg-Strelitz. The Queen had heard of the Schwenkfelders at home, made inquiries concerning them on coming to England, sent greetings to them through Jacob Haagen, a Quaker, and expressed a desire to see their books and know more of them. In 1770 he translated one of Schwenkfeld's tracts on the Christian life for the benefit of Quaker boys who were at his home to study German. In 1771 the *Erläuterung*, or defense of Schwenkfeld and his followers, was issued — to a great extent the work of Christopher Schultz. The *Compendium* or *Glaubenslehre* written out by him was begun in 1775 and finished in 1783 and then allowed to lie in manuscript more than half a century. In 1777 he translated a number of letters on education which had been published in the *Pennsylvania Magazine*, 1775. In 1782 he drew up the constitution of the Schwenkfelder

Society or Church. After subjecting the first edition of his *Catechism* to a severe scrutiny and consequent revision, he issued a second edition in 1784. It may be of interest to quote the following words from Yeakel's *History of the Evangelical Association*, Volume I., page 48 : The Schwenkfelders had " also some very good books, especially an excellent Catechism, of which Rev. William W. Orwig made a liberal use in compiling the second Catechism for the Evangelical Association, published in 1846." A cursory examination shows that in many cases the exact wording was embodied, in others slight variations were made. Singularly the author failed to acknowledge any indebtedness to any one for his Catechism. Christopher Schultz took an active part in the Heintze correspondence and on various occasions came to the defence of the faith in vigorous controversial writings. His sermons at marriages, funerals, and on memorial days, he in many cases wrote out quite fully, and in such shape they are still preserved. A study of his orthography shows that after he had begun his literary work he deliberately changed his system of spelling. While he was thus toiling he also served as pastor, gratis, won his food and raiment and made himself generally useful to the community.

Dr. Abraham Wagner, son of Melchior, was born 1715 (circa) and came to Pennsylvania 1737, where he died 1763. He was an earnest broad-minded Christian and a great reader. He collected poems of John Kelpius, extensive biographical notes on Spener whom he admired and wrote a beautiful letter to Muhlenberg quoted in the *Hallesche Nachrichten*. His poetic productions began before he was 18 and continued to his death. More than fifty of these products are still preserved.

Christopher Wiegner, the diarist, son of Adam Wiegner, was born in Harpersdorf, 1712. During the flight of the Schwenkfelders he was taken to Görlitz, by his parents, where he soon came to take an active part in the religious life of the community. He began to keep a diary or record of his experiences during this time and kept it up until 1739, thus covering the life among the Moravians in Saxony, the migration to Pennsylvania and life in Montgomery county. It furnishes many interesting and authentic details of the momentous period in which he lived. It is to be hoped that ways and means may be found for putting the same into print. For further details see Chapter VIII.

David Schultz, the surveyor, son of George, was born in 1717, came with his father to Pennsylvania in 1733 on account of persecutions and settled in the Goshenhoppen valley where he died, 1797. He wrote an account of the migration to Pennsylvania of the company with which he came published in the *Pennsylvania Magazine of History and Biography*, Vol. X., page 167. He was a great reader and almost incessant writer and in his general relations one of the most important men of his community. He kept a diary in interleaved almanacs that came to light a few years ago and were in part published by the late Henry S. Dotterer in *The Perkiomen Region*. In announcing this publication the editor said: "In the next number of the *Perkiomen Region* we shall commence the publication of a MS. of extraordinary historical interest. It relates especially to the early settlements at Goshenhoppen — old and new, Falkner Swamp, Hereford, Hosensack, Great Swamp, Colebrookdale and Salford, but in a wider sense it furnishes a great amount of authentic information regarding the Colonial period, its people and their

SPECIMEN VOLUMES OF MANUSCRIPT.

WRITTEN AND BOUND BY THE SCHWENKFELDERS IN PENNSYLVANIA.

interests. It is the journal kept by David Shultze, immigrant, colonist, surveyor, scrivener, law adviser, a resident of Upper Hanover township in the Perkiomen Valley. In his journal three languages are employed, German, English and Latin." He wrote a number of poems, one of these on the death of his wife, murdered June, 1750, and scattered notes suggest that he contemplated publishing a book. Rev. C. Z. Weiser wrote these words concerning him: "We have abundant records to show that he had been the recognized scrivener, conveyancer, surveyor and general business agent for the frontier settlers scattered over a wide district in Eastern Pennsylvania as far down as 1797.

Christoph Hoffman son of Balthasar Hoffman was born in 1732 and received a careful religious training at the hands of his father. Between 1758 and 1760 he copied the Weiss hymn book. As a catechist he made record of the work done by him and his class, he wrote an interesting account of his father's life and labors and collected and catalogued his writings in 1795. As minister he delivered sermons on various occasions which are still preserved.

Christoph Kriebel son of Christoph came to Pennsylvania with his parents as a lad of 14 in 1734. In his younger days he copied a number of manuscript volumes. At the religious conference of 1762 he took an active part and read a paper that met with approval by the company. He became a catechist and later a preacher among the Schwenkfelders. As such he wrote out some of his sermons, one series consisting of twenty sermons on the sacraments. He recorded the questions and answers in connection with his Bible classes in four volumes extending from 1764 to 1797. He took a leading part in the

13

Heintze correspondence and made a collection of copies of the more important letters received and sent.

Of the publications relating to the Schwenkfelders the following items may be noted :

1742. *Das kleine A. B. C. in der Schule Christi* — Dr. Abraham Wagner.

1748. *Von dem wahren, ewigen Friedsame Reiche Christi.* George Frell — Germantown, Saur.

1748. *Auszug aus Christian Hohburgs Postilla Mystica* — Saur.

1762. *Neu-Eingerichtetes Gesang-Buch* — Germantown, Saur.

This is a hymn-book 5 x 7, double column, containing xxxiii + 760 pages with three indexes. The book was one of the most ambitious attempts in the line of hymnology in the colony up to that time and must have meant very considerable labor and expense. Christopher Schultz in his *Historische Anmerckungen* says in substance : The printing of a hymn-book for our own use, discussed for some time was regarded desirable because the hymns in use lay scattered, the old printed Picard hymn-books were passing out of use and copying was a tiresome and expensive work. The matter came to an issue in 1759 in such form that a plan was agreed upon and sufficient subscribers declared themselves, and it was decided to proceed with the matter and have the book published. To prepare the manuscript for the printer meant an incredible amount of labor and conferring. The printer began work on it the middle of 1761 and finished the work by the end of 1762. In the introduction are found the following words : " It has been the object to gather beautiful, instructive and edifying hymns. With respect to the beautiful or what may properly be called the beautiful in this connection, but few in

A FEW TITLE PAGES.

our day agree nor would we dispute the taste and judgment of any one. With those however who find the beauty of hymns in the high art of poesy, graceful words and ingenious flowery style or sounds pleasing to the ears, one hopes to win but scant credit through this collection. Such will do well to look for these things not here but elsewhere, though no innocent use of these things is disparaged. For ourselves we chose to aim for what is beautiful before God in order that it may meet his favor and glorify Him. With Him a pure simplicity is an ornament of beauty; this does not mean silliness nor ignorance but a oneness of the heart with God, a condition in which the eye of the mind does not concern itself with what is pleasing to the world, the flesh and evil lusts thereof." This thought influenced their choice of selections and gave tone to their entire work. Sixty authors are represented. The old Bohemian and Moravian hymns sung for many decades by the fathers of the faith received special consideration. They themselves made the following contributions:

Dr. Abraham Wagner, hymns: 6, 7, 10, 14, 96, 109, 139, 173, 191, 281, 283, 365, 457, 478, 495, 711, 733, 742, 751, 756, 787, 754, 789, 800, 802, 821, 822, 826, 832, 833, 845, 847, 850, 463, 801.

Balzer Hoffman, hymns: 1, 253, 303, 309, 310, 319, 320, 350, 351, 352, 353, 354, 355, 374, 383, 571, 572, 578, 579, 580, 581, 588, 589, 617, 618, 626, 627, 628, 705, 709, 710, 755, 792, 854, 855, 856, 458, 573.

Casper Kriebel, hymns: 234, 311, 619, 623, 629, 717, 326.

Christoph Kriebel, hymns: 492, 714, 715, 716, 742, 745, 746, 747.

Christoph Schultz, hymns: 157, 312, 360, 380, 469, 590, 744.

David Seipt, hymn: 673.

George Weiss, hymns: 3, 36, 37, 221, 222, 240, 246, 247, 248, 252, 321, 422, 423, 468, 473, 486, 509, 532, 592, 600, 601, 602, 603, 712, 713, 722, 777.

These constitute 123 numbers, out of a possible 917. By the time the second revision had been finished in 1869, only 26 numbers were regarded worthy of being retained, a result in harmony with the general tendency to drift away from the old moorings.

1763. *Catechismus oder Anfänglicher Unterricht, Christlicher Glaubens Lehre.* Philadelphia, Miller.

1771. *Erläuterung für Herrn Caspar Schwenkfeld, und die Zugethanen seiner Lehre.* Jauer. Heinrich Christ Mullern.

A part of the title page of this book literally translated reads as follows: "An explanation for Casper Schwenkfeld and the adherents of his faith relating to many points in history and theology which commonly are presented incorrectly or passed entirely over, in which their history to 1740 is briefly told, their confessions of faith are summarized and the true conditions of the disputes concerning the ministry, the holy Scriptures and the glory of the humanity of Jesus Christ are unfolded; truthfully and simply described from approved, credible and many hitherto unpublished documents and from personal experience, offered to the service of all seekers after and lovers of the truth by a few of those who sometime ago migrated from Silesia and now reside in Pennsylvania in North America." The necessity for a publication of this kind was felt for some time; consequently in the fall of 1768, it was resolved to issue the book. During the following winter Christopher Schultz prepared the manuscript and by March a printer's copy was in the hands of their friends, the Moravians, to be forwarded to their European correspondent

Heintze at Probsthayn for printing. Heintze received it in October, 1769, and, on application for a royal concession to print, gave the manuscript to the proper officers for examination who did not return the same until July 19, 1770, with the desired authorization to print. The printing of the edition of 500 was finished in April, 1771. Copies were received in Philadelphia in November, 1772, after which they had to be bound by the Schwenkfelder book-binder, Hoffman, before they were ready for general circulation.

1772. *Der Schwenkfelder Glaubens-Bekenntnisz.* Im Jahr 1718. Jauer.

1784. *Kurze Fragen ueber die Christliche Glaubens-Lehre.* Philadelphia, Carl Cist.

1791. *Christliche Betrachtungen ueber die Evangelische Texte.* Durch Erasmum Weichenhan, Germantaun, Michael Billmeyer.

This was a revised edition of the Sultzbach edition of 1672. Propositions had been made to have it printed before the breaking out of the Revolutionary War but on account of this it was put off. Christopher Schultz wrote the sermons for Whitmonday and Ascension Day. He had been instructed even to prepare a postill for the whole church year.

1795. *An Inaugural Botanico-Medical Dissertation on the Phytolacca decandra of Linnæus.* By Benjamin Schultz, of Pennsylvania, Member of the Philadelphia Medical Society. Philadelphia, Thomas Dobson.

1806. *Gebet-Büchlein*, Germantaun. Michael Billmyer.

1813. *Neueingerichtetes Gesangbuch - Philadelphia.* Conrad Zentler. (Revised edition of hymnbook of 1762.)

1816. *Dankbare Erinnerung an die Schwenkfelder in Nord America * * * Görlitz.* Heinze. As a slight token of gratitude for favors shown to their fathers 1726–34, the Schwenkfelders in 1815 gave 163 Reichsthaler to the people of Görlitz and in relief of their sore distress and sufferings due to the ravages of the Napoleonic war. This sixty-four page book was published by the magistrates and councils of Görlitz as a thank offering for the gift.

1819. *Oeconomisches Haus und Kunst-Buch.* Von Johann Krausz. Allentown, Heinrich Ebner.

1819. *Einige Christliche und Lehrreiche Send-Briefe.* Schwenkfeld. Allentown, Heinrich Ebner.

1820. *Von der Himmlische Arzeney.* Schwenkfeld. Allentown, Heinrich Ebner.

1820. An article on the Schwenkfelders was published in the *Amerikanische Ansichten* composed by John Schultz.

1830. *Erläuterung für Herrn Caspar Schwenckfeld.* Sumnytaun, E. Benner. (Revision of edition in 1771.)

1835. *Ein christlicher Send-Brief vom Gebet Schwenkfeld.* Allentown, A. and W. Blumer.

1836. *Compendium von Christoph Schultz, vollendet 1783.* Philadelphia, Schelly and Lescher.

1842. *Christliche Betrachtungen ueber die Evangelische Texte, Erasmus Weichenhan.* Allentown, V. und W. Blumer.

1844. A History of Religious Denominations published by I. Daniel Rupp contains an article on the Schwenkfelders by Isaac Schultz. This was republished in the Desilver History of 1859.

1846. *Lehr Tractate * * * durch Casper Schwenkfeld.* Allentown, Blumer and Busch.

1851. *Constitution * * * wie auch Neben-Gesetze * * * von Josua Schultz.* Allentaun, Guth, Young and Trexler.

1855. *Kurze Fragen über die Christliche Glaubens-Lehre.* Skippackville; J. M. Schünemann. (Third edition of Catechism.)

1858. *Lehr und Ordnungs-Regeln.* Von Josua Schultz. (Date and place of publication not fully established.)

1858. *The Heavenly Balm and the Divine Physician.* By Casper Schwenkfeld, translated by Rev. F. R. Anspach, D.D. Baltimore, published by Abraham Heydrick.

1859. *Fünf Abhandlungen aus den Theologischen Schrifften von Caspar Schwenckfeldt.* Skippackville, J. M. Schünemann & Co.

1860. *Ausführliche Geschichte Kaspar v. Schwenkfelds, und der Schwenkfelder * * * von Oswald Kadelbach.* Lauban, vom M. Baumeister.

1861. *Oeffentliche Correspondenzen Zwischen Josua Schultz und Daniel Weiser, im Jahr 1858 * * ** Lansdale, John Schupe.

1863. *Short questions concerning the Christian Doctrine of Faith, by the Reverend Christopher Schultz.* Translated by Prof. I. Daniel Rupp. Skippackville, J. M. Schünemann.

1869. *Neueingerichtetes Gesang-Buch.* Skippackville, A. E. Dambly.

1870. *Casper Schwenkfeld and the Schwenkfelders.* C. Z. Weiser, in *Mercersburg Review.*

1874. *Schwenkfelders.* By P. E. Gibbons, in *Pennsylvania Dutch.* Philadelphia, J. B. Lippincott & Co.

1875. *Glaubens-Lehren und Bekenntnisse der zwei ersten Predigern der Schwenkfelder in Amerika.*

1876. *Pflicht der Eltern gegen ihre Kinder * * * sammt Einleitung, Trauform, und Gebet.* Skippack, A. E. Dambly.

1876. *Religious Societies of the Commonwealth.* By Barclay. London.

1879. *Genealogical Record of the Descendants of the Schwenkfelders.* By the Rev. Reuben Kriebel, with an historical sketch by C. Heydrick. Manayunk, Josephus Yeakel.

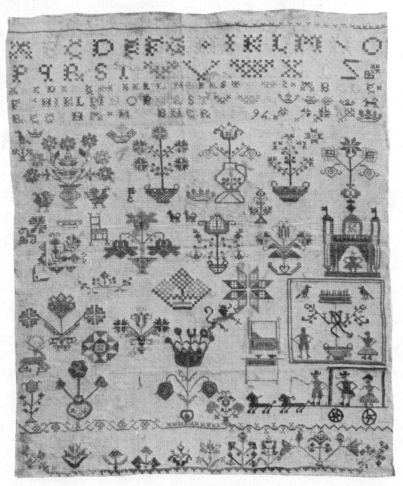

SPECIMEN PENNSYLVANIA-GERMAN SAMPLER.

WROUGHT BY REGINA HEEBNER, 1794.

1882. *Constitution of the Schwenkfelder society as also By-Laws.* Skippack, A. E. Dambly.

1886. *Der Schwenkfelder Glaubens-Bekenntnisz * * * im Jahr 1718.*

1889. *Casper Schwenkfeld.* By Jesse Yeakel, in a German Quarterly.

1894. *Comite Bericht.*

1898. *Formula for the Government and Discipline of the Schwenkfelder Church.* Philadelphia, J. B. Lippincott Co.

1898. *The Schwenkfelders.* By Howard M. Jenkins, in *Friends' Quarterly Examiner.*

1898. *Americana Germanica* published the Historische Anmerckungen and School documents of 1764.

1899. *The Schwenkfelders.* By H. Y. S. (Joseph Henry Dubbs) in *College Student.*

1902. *Formula for the Government and Discipline of the Schwenkfelder Church.* Revised edition. Philadelphia, J. B. Lippincott Co.

Simple justice demands in this connection a reference to the researches and labors of Ober. Lehrer Heinrich August Friedrich Schneider. Born in Posen in 1806, he studied for the ministry but on account of sickness, changed his plans and became teacher of English in the Königliche Real Schule, Berlin in 1842, which place he filled until a nervous trouble compelled him to resign in 1872. His studies in theology led him to read church history and thus he came to be interested in Schwenkfeld before his student days were over. To 1875, when he sold his immense and invaluable Schwenkfeldiana, he devoted all his spare time to this line of study. He published a history of Liegnitz with reference to the Schwenkfelders and an account of early Schwenkfelder hymn writers. He had collected material for an extensive biography of Schwenkfeld. His library was scattered by the sale of 1875, a part being bought by the Hartford Theological Seminary. To his dying day he had a warm heart for his chosen line of study and loved to talk of it.

These remarks may fittingly be brought to a close by a brief reference to the most recent, most elaborate and most exhaustive work in the line of literature relating to the Schwenkfelders. In 1884 the publication of a Corpus Schwenkfeldianorum was undertaken under the editorship of President C. D. Hartranft of the Hartford Theological Seminary. An edition of the works of Schwenkfeld is in preparation which aims to furnish:

1. A critical text, various readings, the original marginalia, explanatory notes and full apparatus. The notes, the preface, the prolegomena, etc., to be in the English language.

2. The chronological order of the documents without regard to encyclopædic arrangement.

3. The text, in smaller type, of all unpublished letters addressed to Schwenkfeld or Crautwald, or that make mention of them. If previously edited, references to the editions will be given in the text. The text of all acts or historical documents hitherto unpublished which refer to them, will be printed in a similar way.

4. The portraits and pictures in connection with the persons in the history, in the year of their appearance.

5. Facsimile specimens of the MSS.

6. A full bibliography of the literature.

7. Indices of persons, places and subject matter to each volume.

8. A history in English of the Reformation by the Middle Way. This is already in course of preparation. Although it is to be published after the text has appeared, it will nevertheless be numbered as the first volume of the series.

CHAPTER XIII.

CONCLUDING REMARKS.

CCORDING to the official notice from the Society the assigned task in the present undertaking was "to write a paper on the Schwenkfelders especially with regard to their history in this Commonwealth." The author could, therefore, not indulge in the pleasant pastime of tracing out and singing the glories of all the lines of descent. To do so would mean at the least a search through Canada and through the northern tier of States beginning with Massachusetts, Connecticut, New Jersey and Maryland, westward through the different commonwealths to the Pacific Ocean. The descendants were and are found in all walks of life — some even having done time in prison cells. An attempt indeed was made at collating a list of prominent descendants, with a view of inserting the same in this history but for a variety of reasons this had to be abandoned. The classification of the skilled professions pursued by these would show eminent lights in callings like the following: Artisans, artists, authors, doctors, editors, inventors, judges, governor, lawyers, legislators, ministers, missionaries, manufacturers, musicians,

merchants, presiding elders, bishops, president and professors of theological seminaries, professors in colleges and
seminaries, teachers, soldiers both in the ranks and as
officers.

The *Genealogical Record of the Descendants of the
Schwenkfelders* published in 1879, a most excellent work
in itself, though not free from error and far from being exhaustive, gives in addition to the Schwenkfelder names of
1734, more than 200 patronymics brought by intermarriage
into connection with the lines of Schwenkfelder descendants.   The descendants of Tobias Hartranft hold family
reunions where hundreds assemble each year.   Of the
descendants of David Wagener who wandered to the Bushkill in Northampton Co., there are hundreds in Easton
alone to-day.   Jemima Wilkinson the religious enthusiast
and impostor, drew David Wagener, the son of Melchior,
to New York, where the descendants are numerous and
prominent.   Settlements in various western states might
also be enumerated.

With respect to church connection, descendants are found
in the Catholic Church and in many branches of the
Protestant church, particularly, United Brethren, Congre-
gational, Evangelical, Lutheran, Reformed, Presbyterian,
Baptist, Methodist, Mennonite and also even in the broad
" Pennsylvania."

Though the present body of " Schwenkfelders " can
claim scant credit for the high honors won by their distant
brotherhood they may at least with them rejoice in the
common pious ancestry and thank God for what He has
done for the children through and on account of the
parents, remembering that the mercy of the Lord is from
everlasting to everlasting upon them that fear Him, and
His righteousness unto children's children.

Appendix.

v. Schwenckfelt.

(205)

Anhang A.

Note by Editor : — For various obvious reasons this letter and the following marriage contract are carefully reproduced as to spelling, etc The italicized words were written in Latin script, the rest in German.

Mein lieber alter Freund *Sebastian!* Es ist mir eine Zeit her offtmals in meinem Gemüth gewesen ich solte dich durch Schreiben etlicher nöthiger Stükke erinnern, dieweil wir lange Zeit so viel ich weis aufrichtige Freunde gewesen sind, damit ich meiner seits doch auch die Pflichten treuer Freundschaft erfüllen, und mich der Schuld entladen möchte derer ich mich durch Schweigen theilhaftig machen würde, und zugleich auch wo möglich dir in deinem Verrennen nützlich seyn möchte. So nihms doch auf (ohne dir weiter viel Umstände vorzumahlen) als von einem alten Freunde, was dir in folgenden Zeilen aus wehmüthigem Hertzen als ein Spiegel vorgehalten wird.

Ich habe mit dir zu Reden als mit einem Mitgliede eines Hauses das den Inwohnern des ehemals freyen **Pennsylvania** Gesetze giebt, und dieselben Gesetze auch durch Gewalt der Waffen, Straffen, Gefängnisse, Ausschlissung aller bürgerlichen Rechte, ohne daß sie ihr Gewissen Rath fragen dürffen, den besagten Inwohnern aufzwinget wie solches nun die letztherige **Test=Acte** bezeuget, und das Verfahren gegen Unschuldige Gewissenhaffte Leute nun hie bey uns ausweiset. So ihr nun als **Representanten** der Einwohner **Pennsylvaniens** wollet angesehen seyn, und von wegen ihrer agiren wollet so habt ihr unumgänglich auch die Pflicht auf euch liegen, daß ihr das wahre wohl aller und jeder Classen besagter Einwohner, so gut als euer Eigenes an eurem Hertzen habt, und nicht die eine Parthey durch Unterdrückung der Andern erhebet, so ferne sie es nicht durch Boßhafftige Untreue oder Lasterhaftigkeit verschuldet. Da du nun gar wohl weissest daß **Pennsyl-**

APPENDIX A.

Draft of Letter by Reverend Christopher Schultz to Sebastian Levan, Member of Assembly, Dated, Hereford, August 12, 1777.

(See page 155.)

(Translation.) *My dear old friend Sébastian:* For some time it has often been in my mind that I ought in writing to remind you of a few necessary points, since for a long time we have been upright friends so far as I know in order that I on my part may fulfill the duties of true friendship and free myself of the blame of which by my silence I would make myself guilty and that at the same time if possible I may be serviceable to you in your erring conduct. Without my further detailing to you many particulars, receive therefore what is held before you mirror-like in the following lines as coming from an old friend out of a sorrowing heart.

I wish to speak with you as with a member of a House which gives laws to the citizens of a once free Pennsylvania and also without taking counsel of their consciences forces these laws upon the said inhabitants by force of arms, fines, imprisonments, exclusion from all civil rights as the recent Test-Act and the proceedings against innocent, conscientious people with us here shows. If you would be looked upon as representatives of the citizens of Pennsylvania and would act in their behalf, you inevitably have the duty resting upon you to take to heart the true welfare of each and every class of said inhabitants as well as your own and not to lift up one party through the suppression of the others in so far as they have not occasioned

(207)

vanien anfänglich das Eigenthum war (beydes in Ansehung des
Landes als auch daß Rechts der Regierung) solcherer Leute, die da
Gewissenhalber bedenken tragen andere Menschen zu tödten; wie
auch sehr bedächtig sind, sich an Eydes Statt in Etwas einzulassen,
woran sie nicht genung gewiß wären daß sie in der Wahrheit und
auch beständig dabey bleiben könnten, und da du zugleich weisest
daß dergl. Leute noch die Menge hie vorhanden sind, ja einen
grossen theil der Ansehnlichsten, und wolgesessenen und Unbeschol-
tenen Einwohnern ausmachen. So fragt man ja wolnothwendig
wenn man eure Acten ansiehet, und zugleich fühlet wie sie appli-
cirt werden. Habt ihr euch den wol jemals in euren Hertzen an
dieser Leute Statt gestellet, und ihre gewissens Angelegenheiten als
eure eigne angesehen und **representirt?** Oder weisets sichs nicht
vielmehr aus daß ihr sie für den nichts werthigsten Auskericht hal-
tet, den ihr aufs äusserste untertretten, und aus dem Lande ver-
dringen woltet? Ists nicht also, warum lieget mein Vetter George
Kriebel in Easton Gefängniß? Und muß sich sagen lassen wenn er
nicht Schwöret wie ihr wollet, so könne er eher nicht heraus kommen, als biß man die Seinen mit Verlassung aller Güter zu den
Feinden überliefert? Warum beraubet ihr uns denn aller Bürgerlichen und Gewissens-Freyheiten, daß nichts mehr soll Unser seyn,
nicht mehr auf Gottes-Erdboden handeln und wandeln dürffen
und also gar nicht leben sollen? bloß allein weil wir bedencken
was zu unser Seelen und Gemüths Ruhe und Frieden dienlich
seyn möge. Weil wir sachen nicht beschwören wolten die jetzt von
äußerster Ungewißheit sind ob wir werden beständig dabey bleiben können, und wir sollen uns doch darüber verschwören. Diß
ist ja doch die Summa von dieser Sache, daß ihr uns hie Sachen
zumuthet und bey Verlust alles was einem in der Welt lieb seyn
kan aufleget, daß nie kein Tyranne ja kein Tartar noch Türke viel-
weniger eine Christliche Regierung in vorigen Zeiten gefordert
hat daß man nemlich unter währender hitzigsten Kriege und vor
Ausgang der Sache, einem vorigen Herren abschwören solte.

it through malicious unfaithfulness or wickedness. Since you indeed know quite well that Pennsylvania was originally the property (both in regard to the land as to the right of government) of those people who on account of scruples of conscience have misgivings against killing other people and who also consider very carefully before entering, in the place of an oath, upon a course concerning which they can not be fully assured that they can continue in the truth and steadfast in it, and as you at the same time know that of these people a large number are still here and constitute a great part of the most respectable, the well-established, and irreproachable citizens. A necessary question when one considers your acts and feels how they are applied is this: — Have you in your hearts at any time put yourself in the place of these people and viewed and represented their matters of conscience as your own? Or is it not shown that you consider them the most worthless sweepings which you wish to suppress to the utmost and crowd out of the land? If this is not the case why is my cousin George Kriebel imprisoned in the Easton jail and must let himself be told that if he does not swear the way you want him to, he can not be set free until his own are delivered to his enemies with abandonment of all his property. Why do you rob us of all civil liberty and freedom of conscience in so much that we are to hold nothing as our own, we are not allowed to trade on God's earth, or move about or even to live — merely because we take into consideration what may be helpful to the rest and peace of our souls and minds; because we are unwilling to take oath concerning things that are of the utmost uncertainty whether we can remain true to the same and yet we are to bind ourselves by oath. This is the sum of the whole matter that you expect things of us in this respect

14

Siehe dich doch in der Historien voriger Zeiten um du wirst nie keine dergleichen Gewissens Tyranney aufweisen können. Ist etwa wegen Spionen, Verräther oder dergleichen **Malefactors** etwas zu thun nöthig gewesen wie das **Preamble** Eurer **Test** Acte saget warum verwickelt ihr denn unschuldige Leute mit dieser ihrer Straffen? Oder wo ist der der uns solcher Händel mit Recht bezeihen kan, las ihn auftretten? Sind wir nicht immer willig gewesen unsere volle Proportion an öffentlichen Lasten zutragen soviel als mit Gewissen, nemlich ohne Rüstung zum Todschlagen seyn kan? Wie komts daß ihr nur immer **Fines** zubenahmen habt, oder daß wirs unterm Tittel **Fine** zu bezahlen haben was von uns gefordert wird? Seyd ihr da unsere getreue **Representanten?**

O mein lieber Freund! Ich bitte dich um Gottes willen bedencke dich weils noch Zeit ist, du magst wohl jetzt dencken, du bist mir ein schöner Freund, daß du mit so groben Fragen an mich kommest. Aber Aber es bleibt dir fürwahr nicht aussen, und ich wünsche deiner Seelen von Hertzen daß es nicht zu spät geschehe, du wirst vor deme deme wir alle Rechenschafft geben müssen einmal theuer antworten müssen, ob du Ihme auch Die Seinen mit Unterdrückung berührt habest, die nemlich ihre Hoffnung und Vertrauen auf Ihn stellen, die sich scheuen Ihn zu beleidigen, und die sich fürchten für seinem Wort.

Ihr seyd nun auf das Militz Wesen so erpicht, als wenns der eintzige Schutz wäre der uns Salviren könne, und alles andere wird mit höchster Verachtung ja Straffe angesehen. Nun du wirst dich doch auch noch erinnern können, daß wir gehöret haben, daß alles in der Hand des Höchsten stehet, und daß man sich seinem Schutz von gantzem Hertzen solte anvertrauen, denn er könne und solle Schützen alle die zu ihm fliehen, und verlassen sich nicht auf ihre Stärke. Wolan wers nun von Hertzen Treu und Redlich mit seinem Lande meynet; Wohin ja wohin und zu was soll ein solcher in dieser jammerlich bedrängten Zeit fliehen oder was vor

and impose them upon us with loss of all that one holds
dear in the world, things that no tyrant, nor tartar nor turk
much less a Christian government in former times demanded, namely that in the midst of the hottest warfare
and before the conclusion of the matter a former lord is to
be denied under oath. Consider the history of former
times and you will not be able to show a like tyranny over
conscience. If action indeed was necessary with respect
to spies, traitors or the like malefactors as the preamble of
your Test Act declares, why do you implicate innocent
people in their punishment? Or where is he who can
justly accuse us of such things? let him step forth. Have
we not always been willing to bear our full proportion of
the public burdens as far as might be done conscientiously,
that is without preparation for manslaughter. Why is it
that you are continually speaking of fines or, that what is
demanded of us must be paid under the name fine? Are
you here our true representatives?

O my dear friend! I beseech you for God's sake, consider while it is yet time. You may indeed now think,
you are a nice friend that you come to me with such un-
civil questions. But, but you will indeed not escape, and
I heartily wish for the sake of your soul that it may not
be too late, that you will have to answer dearly before
him before whom we must all render account, whether
you have oppressed God's own who place their hope and
trust in Him, who are afraid to offend Him and who fear
his word.

You are now so passionately attached to the militia system, as if it were the only protection that could save us
and all else is looked down upon with the highest contempt and even punishment. You can doubtless still recall that we have heard that all things are in the hands of

Rüstung soll er am förderſten gebrauchen und ſich drein einkleiden oder wie thut er am beſten **exerciren.**

Mein lieber Freund! Stelle dirs doch einmal eine viertel Stunde alſo vor; Du ſäheſt einem in ſeinem verborgenen Winckel liegen vor ſeinem Gott mit heiſſen Thränen ſein und ſeines Volckes Sünden den groſſen Herrſcher beichten und bekennen und um des einiges Verſöhners und Mittlers willen vor das Land um Barmhertzigkeit und Verſchonen flehen, ja um die Erneuerung und Beſſerung der Hertzen aller Inwohner der auch aus dem Gefühl der mitleidenden Liebe, da Gott alle Menſchen liebet, ihnen Leben und Odem giebet, keinem Neben = Menſchen das Leben nehmen wolte. Du ſäheſt aber auf der andern Seite einen unſeren gewöhnlichen Militz=Pürſchen er ſey Officier oder Gemeiner in ſeiner ordinairen Poſitur wie die meiſten ſich aufziehen und ſeine Militäriſchen Geſchäfte ausrichten, wie weit unſere Militzen reichen; da möchte ich denn gerne deines Gewiſſens urtheil hören, welches von dieſen beyden der beſte Landes = Beſchützer ſey? Ich urtheile jener thut ſo viel zum wahren Schutz als von dieſen eine gantze **Batallion** nicht ausrichtet, und wer weiß ob dies nicht anklopfet daß du mir ſchier recht geben ſolteſt? Und mir iſts als wenn ich dir ſagen dorffte ohne daß du gar viel an der Wahrheit zweifelteſt ſolcher Art Landesbeſchützer giebts noch in unſerm armen Pennſylvanien die mit ihrem exercieren zwar kein Weſen noch Aufſehens machen die aber eigentlich der Höchſte in ſeiner Rolle hat und ihm wolbekannt ſind, daß ſie zu ſeinem Heerlager gehören, der zählet ihre Thränen und faſſet ſie in ſein Sack.

O hüte dich mein lieber Sebaſtian, hüte dich, daß du keinem von dieſen Landes=Vätern und Streittern des Herren einiges Leyd zufügeſt, wie ich leyder Vermuthe daß mit etlichen eurer letztheriger Acten geſchehen iſt, wer gegen ſie angehet hats mit ihren Herren zu thun. Denn ich muß mein Vermuthen nicht verhalten daß nemlich dieſer Vortrefflichen Art Leute, mehr auf der Seite zu finden ſind die eure Acten und Straffen belegen, weder auf der Seite ſo

the Highest and that one ought to entrust himself wholly into His care, since he can and will protect all who flee to him and do not depend on their own strength.

Now then, whoever holds true and honest intentions concerning his country, whither, yea, whither, and to what shall such a one flee in the present pitiable, distressful times or with what armor shall he shield or clothe himself or what is the best way of "exercising" for him? My dear friend, imagine for a quarter of an hour the matter in this way; you see one lying in his secret chamber before his God with hot tears confessing and acknowledging the sins of himself and his people to the great ruler and pleading for mercy and forbearance in behalf of his land through the only atoner and mediator, yea, for the renewal and betterment of the hearts of all inhabitants and who out of the feelings of compassionate love because? God loves all men and gives them life and breath, would not take the life of any fellowman. On the other side you see one of our ordinary militia fellows, be he officer or private, in his ordinary posture as the most of them pose and performing his military services as far as our militia reach. I should like to hear the judgment of your conscience which of the two is the best protector of his country? I judge the former does more for true protection than a whole battalion of the latter can accomplish and who knows but that this appeals to you that you must admit that I am right. And I feel that I may say to you without your seriously doubting the truth of it that of this class of defenders of the country some are still to be found in our poor Pennsylvania who indeed make no ado or sensation with their "exercising" but whom the highest has in books and who are well-known as belonging to his army, who also counts their tears and puts them into his bottle.

der Drommel folgen. Ich sage mehr, dabey ich den letztern ihren Antheil nicht abstreiche. Ich will nur sagen ein wahrer **Representant** des Landes hat sich von Gott und Gewissens ja Recht und Billigkeit wegen derer Einwohner die Gewissenshalbe in allerley Thätlichkeiten nicht eingehen so treu und sorgfältig anzunehmen sowol als derer andern; und die Gewissens=Freyheit ist ihnen auch durch öffentliche **Acta** und **Pacta** so Eigenthümlich, daß sie ihnen nicht kan entwendt werden ohne den schnödesten Raub zu begehen.

Eine freywillige Militz lasse ich in ihrem gehörigen Werthe, als auch von Leuten deren Anliegen gehöret **estimirt** und **representirt** zu werden, aber das bißherige betreiben des Militz Wesens ist leyder mehr eine Quelle unversönlichen Hasses, Neydes und schädlicher uneinigkeit gewesen weder daß es unsere Umstände gebessert hätte, und hat zugleich das Land in gar Ungeheure Schulden gereumet; ja wie ich finde so ist es die Verhinderung daß eine stehende Armee nicht hinlänglich hat mögen zustande gebracht werden können. Wovon ein jeder Vernünftiger von Anfang leicht hat sehen können, daß wo Krieg geführet werden muß, so kan nur durch diese nicht aber durch die Militz etwas namhafftes ausgeführet werden, und da hätten auch alle Einwohner Hübsch gleich Antheil und ohne vorwurff tragen können. Aber das innerliche Verderben unter uns selbst solte uns fressen. Da ist dieses ein geschikkt Instrument dazu. Da nimmt man einem mit Trotz und Gewalt £25 sammt Unkosten so viel als man will und giebts Einem der vor 8 Wochen Dienst annehmen will und giebt ihm noch £5 beyseits. Wo werden nun die Thoren zu finden seyn die für 20 Thaler auf 3 Jahr Dienst nehmen da einem bey solchem Militz betreiben in einem Jahr £150 werden können? Wenn solch Ding dem Lande nicht **Ruin** bringet, so weiß ich nicht was es nicht ertragen könte. Allein diese Treiber verlassen sich darauf daß die guten Leute nicht wieder fechten werden und fahren hoch her. Aber der Höchste wird sie schon wissen zu finden.

Von der **Test=Acte** weisets nun hie die Erfahrung und das Ge

O, guard yourself, my dear Sebastian, guard yourself that you may not cause any sorrow to any of these fathers of the land and warriors of the Lord as I, alas, surmise has happened through several of your recent acts — whoever assails them must reckon with their Lord. For I must not withhold my suspicion, namely, that of this excellent class of people more are to be found on the side of those who condemn your acts than on the side of those who follow the drum. I say more in order that I may not deprive the latter of their share. I will merely say that a true representative of the land must espouse before God and conscience, yea for the sake of right and propriety the cause of those inhabitants who on account of scruples of conscience do not enter into all the activities as honestly and carefully as that of the others, and freedom of conscience is theirs so specifically by public acts and agreements that they can not be deprived of it without the most iniquitous robbery.

To a voluntary militia I will concede its proper value as being also of people whose solicitude deserves to be esteemed and represented. The management of the militia hitherto prevailing has, alas, been a source of irreconcilable hatred, envy and injurious discord much more than a cause of improvement of our condition and at the same time has cast the land into enormous debts and as I learn it has been the hindrance that a standing army could not be adequately established. Any person of reason could easily foresee from the beginning that where war must be carried on, telling work can only be accomplished by these but not through the militia and here happily all citizens could without offence have taken part. But internal destruction amongst ourselves was to devour us and this has become a fitting instrument thereto. Twenty-five pounds

fühl daß dadurch aller Boßheit, Frevel, Raub und Muthwillen Thür und Thor angeln weit aufgethan ist, solchen an der stillen unschuldigen gewissenhafften Leuten ohne Scheu und Scham in diesem unserm Werthen Lande auszuüben, ja etliche der Vorsteher der Gesetzen laden die ihres gleichen Sinnes zum Unrecht sind wol öffentlich dazu ein, Gott Erbarme es und Steure doch den Frevel! Soll nicht die Obrigkeit Gottes Statt hie Vertretten der an der Tugend einen Wolgefallen und an aller Untugend einen Greuel hat? Ja ist sie nicht zum Schutz der Frommen und zur Straffe der Bösen eingesetzt? Solches wird er dereinst in aller Strenge von ihren Seelen fordern, der da aller Welt Richter ist in Gerechtigkeit.

Keine **Freeholder** sind wir nicht mehr; Für keine Zeugen lassen sie uns nicht mehr gelten; von unserm Lande sollen wir nicht schreiten bis man uns zum **Howe** oder in die Wilde See jaget; Ein jeder mag uns schlagen, geisseln, verhöhnen, tractiren wie der Satan es ihm eingeben kan so finden wir bey jetziger Obrigkeit keine Hülffe noch Schutz anders als daß sie uns in sicheres Gefängniß stekkt daselbst zu verschmachten. Und das alles darum daß wir durch einen öffentlichen Eyd, oder an Eydes Statt das nicht versprechen oder beschweren wollen, was wir nicht wissen können ob wirs möglich werden halten können, und also ohne Gewissens Beflekkung nicht geschehen kan.

O überdencke doch diese Sachen und mercke um Gottes willen was ihr gemacht habt, und ändert ehe die Hand des Höchsten euch erhaschet und ohne Scheuen drein schlagen thut. Ob ich nun gleich um das meinige käme so wolte ich doch nicht um 10 deiner kostbaren Estaten meine Hand in diesen ungerechten Händeln haben. Ich gehe Morgen nach **Philadelphia** um zu sehen ob diesen Unrath von dort aus nicht kan Einhalt geschehen, denn so können wir nicht leben. Inzwischen habe ich dich noch einst solch gestalt erinnern wollen denkest du ich wäre in etwa unrecht dran, so weise mich doch auch in freundschafft des bessern an, ich werde es in aller Liebe an-

GROUP OF SCHWENKFELDER NONOGENARIANS.

SAMUEL YEAKEL,
1798-1887.
GEORGE ANDERS.
1798-1890.
MRS. SARAH ALTHOUSE.
1811-1903.

MRS. REGINA NEWMAN.
1798-1889.
DAVID HEEBNER.
1810-1890.
GEORGE SCHULTZ.
1801-1895.

MRS. CHRISTINA KRAUSS.
1787-1877
MRS. SUSANNA STAHL.
1807-1899
SAMUEL KRAUSS.
1807.

JOHN KRAUSS.
1813-1903.

CHRISTOPHER YEAKEL.
1784-1874.

with expenses are by force and violence taken from one
and given to another who will accept eight weeks' service
with an additional bounty of five pounds. Where may
the fools be found who would accept twenty dollars on three
years' service when by such military economy £150 may
be had in a year? If such things will not bring ruin to
our country, I do not know what it may not endure. These
inciters count on it that the good people of the land will
not fight against them, but the Highest will know how to
punish them.

Concerning the Test Act, experience and sentiment show
that by it door and gate are opened wide to all manner of
vanity, robbery, iniquity and mischief to carry out the same
on quiet, innocent, conscientious people without fear or
shame in this our worthy land, yea, several of the execu-
tives of the laws publicly encourage in such conduct those
who with them are equally inclined to wrong-doing. May
God have mercy and restrain the iniquity. Shall not the
government here take the place of God to whom virtue is
well-pleasing and all vice an abomination. Yea, is it not
established to protect the good and to punish the evil? For
this their souls will be called to account at the great day in
all strictness by him who is the judge of the whole world in
righteousness.

We are freeholders no more; as witnesses we are accepted no more; we are not to step from our own land lest
we be driven to Howe or into the wild sea; Every one may
beat, scourge, deride, abuse us as Satan can inspire him
and we shall receive from the present government no help
nor protection other than that we are placed in secure imprisonment there to languish. And all this because we
will not by public oath or its substitute promise or vow that
which we do not know whether we are able to fulfill and

nehmen, der ich noch verharre, dein Liebe schuldiger Freund und wolwünscher. Hereford d. 12. Aug. 1777.

Chr. Schultz.

P. S.   Wenn du gerne wilst so sende mir mit dem Ueber-bringer dieses **David Meschter** meine zwei Büchlein wieder die ich dir einmal Lehnens Weise brachte; da wir noch freye Leute wa-ren; Aber nach den jetzigen Rechten darff ich dir sie nicht wieder-fordern.   Sey von mir samt deinem Weibe hertzlich gegrüsset **Vale.**

hence can not be done without pollution of conscience. O, consider these things and for God's sake reflect what you have done and change it before the hand of the Highest overtakes you and fearlessly punishes you. Were I even to lose my own, I would not for ten such rich estates as yours be partaker in these unrighteous actions. To-morrow I shall go to Philadelphia to see whether from that quarter restraint of this iniquity may be had for thus we can not live. In the meantime I wished in this way to call your attention to these things. If you think I have erred in any respect in friendliness show me what is better and I shall accept it in love.

I remain

your friend and well wisher

CHR. SCHULTZ.

Hereford, Aug. 12, 1777.

P. S. If it be agreeable to you, send with the messenger who delivers this, David Meschter, my two books again which I brought you at one time by way of a loan when we were still free people, but according to present rights I may not ask them again of you. Hearty greetings to you and your wife. Vale.

Anhang B.

Von der Befragung, so die Hauß=Väter nöthig achten, an die=
jenige zu thun, so die Trauungen unter uns begehren geleistet zu
haben.

Der Herr lasse es ihm wohlgefallen, und zu seiner Ehr gerei=
chen.

Nachdem unsere Vorfahren und Eltern, so Schwenckfelder ge=
nannt, in Deutschland, sich mit keiner Parthey in der Lehre haben
können vergleichen noch vereinigen, und also wegen derselbigen
vieles Ungemach erleiden und erdulden müssen, die Lehr auch nicht
öffentlich pflegen dürfften, und ihnen endlich gar kein Zuflucht=Ort
mehr zugelassen wurde. So entschlossen sie sich, hierein nach
Pennsylvanien (auf Nachricht der Gewissens=Freyheit allhier) zu
gehen, welches sie Anno 1734 gethan. Und weilen die Lehre dazu
sie sich, und auch wir uns noch bekennen, das eintzige Haubt=Stücke
ist, was uns von andern Völckern unterscheidet, und also uns hie=
mit zu einem besondern (oder von andern abgeschiedenem) Volcke
macht: So gebührets uns daß wir Hauß=Väter, jetzund noch (wie
damahls unsere Vorfahren) uns bey allen angelegentlichen Vorfäl=
len (also auch beym Vorfall der Trauung) die Lehr niemahls sol=
ten aus unserm Haubt=Gemercke kommen lassen. 1. Um dieser
bißher noch so ädlen und zur Lehr-Uebung dienenden Gewissens=
Freyheit wegen, nach welcher wir auch berechtigt sind, die Ehe=Voll=
ziehung unter uns selbst zu thun. 2. Um Gottes Ehre willen, die
durch reine Lehr soll gefördert werden. 3. Um unserer Erbau=
ung. 4. Um dieselbe bey unsern Nachkommen aufrecht zu erhal=
ten, als auch ihnen zu einem guten Exempel. Um 5 auch um Got=
tes wegen, da er wol ein solches von uns erwarten mag, daß wir
die Lehre gemeinschäfftl. als auch daheim für sich fleissig übten und
damit vor jedermänniglich beweisen, daß es uns auch was sonder=

APPENDIX B.

MARRIAGE CONTRACT, OCTOBER 1779. (See page 73.)

(Translation). Account and statement of the examination which the housefathers regard necessary to be held of those who make request to have the marriage ceremony performed among us.

May it be well-pleasing to the Lord and redound to his honor.

Our forefathers and parents in Germany called Schwenk-felders could reconcile and unite themselves in doctrine with no party and in consequence had with respect to the same to endure and suffer much inconvenience, could not publicly foster their doctrines and finally were even not allowed a place of refuge. They, therefore, resolved (on hearing of freedom of conscience here) to migrate to Pennsylvania which they did in the year 1734. And since the doctrine which they confessed as we yet do is the only principal article which differentiates us from other people and thus makes us a people, distinct or separate from others, it is becoming that we housefathers even now yet (as our forefathers then) should in all important events (as also in the case of marriage) permit doctrine at no time to cease to be our distinguishing mark.

1. On account of the liberty of conscience hitherto prevailing, so precious and serviceable to the culture of doctrine, according to which we are also permitted to perform the marriage ceremony among ourselves.

2. On account of the glory of God which is to be advanced by pure doctrine.

3. On account of our own edification.

(221)

bares und angelegenes sey, derentwegen von andern Völckern un=
terschieden zu sehn. Daher man sich verpflichtet befunden, und
noch befindet, diejenigen so die Trauung bey uns begehrt geleistet
zu haben, und fernerhin begehren möchten, sie nicht so platt, abzu=
weisen, um sie auch hiemit nicht von der Lehre weg zu lenken, noch
uns selbst schämlich vor Gott und Menschen darzustellen, als nicht
achtende auf Lehre und zusammen dienen daher haben wir es für
nöthig geachtet, daß wir sie in Kürtze, auf folgende zwey Fragen
ersuchten und aufs Gemercke der Lehr leiteten, und zwar vornehm=
lich den Bräutigam wie folgt. 1. Ob er sich auch wol bedacht, ge=
prüfft und untersuchet habe, daß es ihm um Gottes Ehre und der
eigenen Heyls wegen um unsere Lehre zu thun sey (die ihm doch
nun nicht unbekannt seyn werde) und daß er solche aus eigenem
untersuchen und Begriffe für richtig halte, und folglich aus freyem
Willen, und ungezwungenem Gemüthe sich an solche anschließen
und zustimmen könne, so daß er sich, vor sich selbst und die Seinen
derselben nach Gottes verleyen ins künfftige treulich halten und
dieselbe mit sammt den andern wolle helffen pflegen und unter=
stützen? Und ob seine verlobte auch eigentlich eines solchen Willens
sey?

Und weil nach den Landes=Gesetzen, eine vorgesetzte Person,
die Träuungen verrichten muß, und wir aber keine haben; Ob er 2
sich auch zu dem entschliessen könte, wenn künfftig hin, ein und ande=
rer, auch in dergleichen Angelegenheiten wie er gegenwärtig, möchte
kommen und ein solches unter uns und von uns, begehrte ihm ge=
meinschafftlich mit den andern wolle suchen durch zu helffen, und
einen Hauß=Vater helffen anstimmen, dem es übergeben würde,
die Trauung zu thun?

Wenn denn einfältig und treulich auf diese zwey Fragen ge=
williget und zugestimmet worden, so hat mans für billig geachtet,
einem solchen zu willfahren, dabey man das beste gehoffet, indem
man niemanden ins Hertze sehen kan. Hierauf hat man noch für
nützlich gehalten ihnen anzurathen (wie auch von Alters her beym

4. To maintain the same among our posterity and to give them a good example.

5. For God's sake also who may indeed expect of us that we shall both jointly and also privately at home cultivate the same and thus show before every one that it is to us a serious and notable matter to be in this regard a people separate from others.

Wherefore, we have found ourselves obligated both in the past and the present with regard to those who desire to have the marriage ceremony performed among us, and in the future may desire, not to turn these so flatly aside and thus direct them away from the doctrine and also show ourselves to our shame before God and man as not regarding our doctrine and not working together.

We have, therefore, regarded it necessary by the following two questions to appeal to them and in particular to the groom and direct their attention to doctrine as a distinguishing mark. 1. Whether he had carefully reflected, weighed and examined himself that he earnestly took to heart the glory of God, his own salvation and our own doctrine (that would indeed not be unknown to him) and that as a result of his own investigation and understanding he regards the same as correct and hence of his free will and unconstrained mind can attach himself and give assent to the same so that he for himself and his own by God's grace will in the future help to cultivate and support the same? And whether his betrothed for herself also gives assent to the same?

And since by the laws of the country an appointed person must perform the ceremony and we have none. 2. If in the future some one or other under circumstances similar to his own should come and request the same of and by us whether he could assent to this, that he would in com-

Chriſten-Volcke geſchehen) daß die Braut-Leute, von dem der ſie
trauen ſolte, ſich vorhero noch von ihm aus Chriſtlicher Lehr liſſen
befragen und unterrichten.   Zu welchem, ſo bißher nach obigem
Innhalt eingewilliget, auch hierzu, wie billich, alle verſtanden
haben.   Welche aber bißher der Pflegung der Lehr nicht beyge-
wohnt, und gleichwol ſolchen Dienſt zu leiſten von uns begehret,
da haben ſich die Hauß-Väter, den Bräutigam was mehr zu befragen verpflichtet befunden um zu erfahren wie es um ſeine Ange-
legenheit zur Lehr ſtehet.   Wer ſich nun aber bey ſeiner bevorſte-
henden Träuung zu obiger Befragung nicht verſtehen kan, da können wir uns auch nach Landes-Geſetzen und Chriſtlicher Verfaſſung
nicht befugt achten uns mit ihm zu ſolchem wichtigen öffentlichen
Handel einzulaſſen.

Solches bezeugen die Hauß-Väter ſowol alte als junge, mit
ihrer eigenen Hand.

Chriſtoph Schultz.
Chriſtoph Jäckel.
George Wigner.
Johan Jäckel.
Melchior Schultz.
Chriſtoph Kribel.
Chriſtoph Hoffman.
Melchior Kribel, jun.
David Kriebel.
Abraham Dreſcher.
Abraham Jäckel.
Abraham Kriebel.
Hanß Chriſtoph Hübner.
George Kriebel.
George Anders.
George Heydrich.
George Kriebel.
Chriſtoph Meſchter.
Melchior Jäckel.
Abraham Schultz.
Baltzer Kraus.

Georg Jäckel.
Chriſtopher Schultz, jun.
Casper Jäckel.
Jacob Jäckel.
Gregorius Schultz.
Matthäs Gerhardt.
Jeremias Jäckel.
Andreas Schultz.
George Dreſcher.
David Schultz.
Baltzer Schultz.
George Schultz.
Andreas Kriebel.
Abraham Kribel.
Jeremias Kriebel.
Chriſtoph Jäckel Küffer.
Melchior Schubert Kiefer.
Abraham Heirich.
Chriſtoph Meiſchter.
David Schultz.

mon with the others befriend such a one and help to select a housefather to whom the performance of the marriage ceremony might be entrusted.

These two questions having been sincerely and honestly agreed and assented to, it was deemed in place to accede to the request of such a one in hope for the best since no one can see into the heart. Hereupon it was also considered salutary to advice them (as was the custom among Christian people in earlier times) that those engaged to be married should beforehand be catechized and instructed by the one who was to marry them. To the foregoing hith erto approved as given above all have appropriately given assent. In case of those who did not hitherto support our doctrines and who yet made request to have such service rendered by us, the housefathers found themselves under obligation to question the groom somewhat more fully to determine how much he was concerned about our doctrine. If any one can, however, not consent to the above questions in the matter of his approaching marriage we can not consider ourselves authorized by the laws of the Land and Christian organization to enter upon such an important public act with him.

The housefathers both old and young bear testimony to the above in their own handwriting.

15

INDEX.